EFFECTIVE INTERVIEWING

EFFECTIVE INTERVIEWING

John Fletcher

Published in Association with
The Institute of Chartered Accountants
in England and Wales

KOGAN
PAGE

First edition, entitled *The Interview at Work*, published by Duckworth 1973
Second edition published by The Dolphin Puppeteers Limited 1986
Third edition, entitled *Effective Interviewing*, published in 1988 by Kogan Page
Limited, 120 Pentonville Road, London N1 9JN

British Library Cataloguing in Publication Data
Fletcher, John, *1929-*
    Effective interviewing. — 3rd ed.
    1. Personnel. Interviewing – Manuals
    I. Title II. Fletcher, John, *1929 –*
    Interview at work
    658.3′1124

ISBN 1-85091-618-7
ISBN 1-85091-619-5 Pbk

Typeset by Wordbook Ltd, London
Printed and bound in Great Britain by
Biddles Ltd, Guildford

Contents

Preface

There are long books about interviewing, particularly interviewing for recruitment, and there are chapters about interviewing in books on other subjects. This book is meant to fill
the gap between the two.

It is based on my experience of running courses in interviewing for industry and the Civil Service. It should therefore
be of practical value to the manager and administrator. My hope
is that it is not just more background reading for managers, but
that it will serve the manager faced with a difficult interview,
who should read the appropriate part of the book and check
through the notes. It is also intended for students taking
professional examinations in Communication, and for those
teaching the subject. The role-plays in Chapter 5 presuppose
classroom study; they are written for post-experience students
on in-company courses, but with a few amendments to the
roles, all can play.

Some people object to the idea that interviews can be divided
up into grievance, instruction, correction, and so forth. They
point out that real interviews often cut across these arbitrary
dividing lines. Well, sometimes they do and sometimes they
don't, and sometimes they do because there is a muddle. But
it seems to me that there is a lot to be said for looking at
different kinds of interview separately, even if the separation
is theoretical. You are more likely to be able to steer a car
and change gear simultaneously if, when you were learning, you
practised steering in one lesson and changing gear in another.

Many of the individuals and organisations with whom I have
worked will recognise some contribution of their own. I thank
them all, though I cannot name them all, for the ideas and help
they have given. I should like specifically to acknowledge the
guidance of the late Tom Fassam, who was the ideal teacher.
When he was my boss, he used to say of some operation: "If
it goes well, you take the credit; if it goes badly, the blame is
mine." (If all managers followed his example, instead of doing the
opposite, how different the world would be.) Now I can return

the compliment. If anything in the book is creditable, the credit is probably due to him. For its faults I alone am to blame.

Chapter 1
Principles of Interviewing

1. Definition of "interview"

An interview is a meeting of two people, face to face, to accomplish a known purpose by discussion.

This is the definition implied in this book, except for a short look into the panel selection interview, which involves more than two people.

In most of the interviews discussed the two people are a subordinate and a boss. We are concerned with the interview "at work", but the principles apply elsewhere.

If you remove from this definition all reference to a purpose, what is left defines a conversation. A conversation with a purpose, a known purpose, becomes an interview. These definitions are not just games with words; the fact is that interviews can become conversations if the purpose is forgotten.

Much of the awe that surrounds the interview would disappear if it were called a purposeful conversation. Human beings converse merrily from an early age, and develop skills in conversing. They discover what amuses and what does not. They learn how to recognise the non-verbal signals in a conversation, and how to handle difficult people and difficult subjects. All this is valuable preparation for interviewing. True, some people are not "good conversationalists"; usually this means that they cannot readily think of things to say. This should be no problem to an interviewer, because the known purpose fixes the subject. If there is nothing more to be said to the purpose, the interview should end.

Some of the unjustified assumptions made about interviews would disappear. People have purposeful conversations on buses, in a workshop, or on their way to or from the canteen, but tend to think of an interview as something that must be in an office. But the good interviewer asks where the best place is, and considers

9

some alternatives to the office. A car, a pub or a park may be more successful.

The word "formal" comes in here. It is often used to categorise interviews, but unfortunately it is ambiguous, and in discussing the interview, this leads to misunderstanding. A "formal" interview may be

1. an interview with a purpose and a plan;
2. an interview held by appointment and at an agreed place;
3. an interview of which a written record is kept, as with a "formal reprimand".

There are doubtless other meanings in the phrase "a formal interview". Just to show how confusing the terms can be, many organisations keep a written record of an interview officially called an "informal" reprimand. "Formal" and "informal" are not much use unless those who use the phrases also say which kind of "formal" they mean. All the interviews we are concerned with now are formal in sense 1, as they have a purpose by definition and a plan to achieve the purpose. They are not necessarily formal in sense 2, and only the exceptional cases will be formal in sense 3.

2. Summary notes

Aims
1. To improve the performance of the boss, the subordinate, or the organisation generally
2. To test or improve morale, attitudes and feelings
3. To get information
4. To give information
5. To enable the subordinate (not the boss) to let off steam, to release pent-up emotion
6. To analyse a question, solve a problem, or specify recommendations
7. To implement the policy of senior management
8. To remove difficulties or clear up misunderstandings
9. To find out how successful a previous interview was.

Preparation
Preparation is necessary, even if it has to be done by thinking

quickly during the first few minutes of the interview.

1. Clear your mind about the purposes of the interview

Do not try to do something which would be better done in some other way, such as a large meeting or a circular

Do not set yourself a purpose which you cannot achieve in the time

Do not try to do a job which is really someone else's.

2. Study the subject or subjects

Get necessary information or facts

Give advance information if necessary

Note the main points to be dealt with

Anticipate probable conflicts of opinion, interest or value.

3. Estimate how long the interview will last

4. Outline a plan for the discussion

Think out the opening statement

Consider opening questions

Plan intermediate phases, with timings if necessary

Build up a picture of the final summary, with conclusions and action if necessary, but be prepared to modify these as the interview proceeds

If "problem-solving", consider the alternative solutions which may be proposed

Make notes of the plan, to refer to in the interview.

5. Have everything ready

Choose a suitable place

Ensure privacy and eliminate distractions

Prepare supporting documents, pen, and paper

Give adequate warning if appropriate.

Structure

1. Introduce the subject or subjects

State the topic in a few words

Indicate the time available

Provide the essential information:
  Background
  Facts
  Main points
Clarify the purpose and scope of the interview:
  Friendly
  Official
  Confidential to whom
Outline the sequence of the interview (a "logical pathway")
Open the discussion with a carefully framed question.

2. Guide the discussion
Adjust the degree and nature of control as the interview develops
Draw out information, facts, experience, opinions and suggestions
Distinguish and assemble these in an orderly arrangement
Restate them in your own words
Ensure that the interviewee understands and accepts your restate-
  ment
Clear up misunderstandings
Keep discussion on the subject, without intimidating the inter-
  viewee
Break up "circular" sequences, retreading old ground
Distinguish facts from opinions and inferences
Separate feeling from reasoning
Discourage personal remarks or arguments, usually by ignoring
  them
Encourage the interviewee to talk
Make full use of stimulating questions
Keep an eye on the time, but as unobtrusively as possible.

3. Clarify and crystallise progress
Summarise each phase of the interview
State intermediate conclusions
Clarify points of agreement and disagreement
Check that summaries are understood and agreed.

4. Establish results of interview
Give final summary
State what has been agreed, and what must still be resolved

Say if a further interview is needed, and when
State conclusions
State action to be taken, if any
Check that these are understood and accepted.

5. Check results
Ask how you will discover whether the interview was successful
Check the aims set for the interview with the actual consequences
If the interview was not entirely successful, ask yourself whether
   this is for reasons outside the interview. If not, how could the
   interview have been more successful? Where did you go wrong?

3. Status

The rights and obligations of people are recognisable before
the interview begins. They should be maintained throughout the
interview, and should not (except in an obvious case like promotion)
be affected by the interview.

The smooth conduct of interviews depends on the rights and
obligations given by the organisation: in other words, it depends
on the status of the participants. Work cannot be done efficiently
if it is not clear who is responsible for what, or who is responsible
to whom for what. Relationships arise out of responsibility.

Attempts to undermine the allocation of responsibility defeat the
purpose of the interview. A boss who begins, "Of course, I know
it's all nonsense, but senior management have said they want the
job done" will forfeit the respect of the subordinate, will create the
feeling that "A boss who has so little loyalty to senior management
cannot expect my loyalty", and the job will probably be badly done.
The subordinate knows the boss does not think it is worth doing,
and if senior managers object, it is the boss who will be answerable,
not the subordinate. Delegation is admirable and necessary but it
does not diminish the authority or responsibility of the boss over
the subordinate. Ultimately the actions of subordinates can get
a boss into trouble.

Status gives security; it establishes where people stand. This
may be why interviews are more difficult in large impersonal
organisations, with a continual change of staff, than in a small family
firm, where there is always a starting point for the interview in the

13

clear roles and status of those concerned. Status is the framework of decisions, and the drive behind carrying out decisions.

4. Truth and sincerity

The idea of a manager's social responsibility is gaining ground. Problems of the environment, of honesty in advertising, of discrimination in employment, are all part of a manager's worries. It is not just pious opinion which says this, or even public opinion; managers themselves find that their most difficult problems are those involving moral or ethical matters. It is not a case of having to choose between the selfish course and the honest one. Often it is a conflict of loyalties; the manager has to choose between loyalty to one group (say a superior or the customers) and loyalty to another group (say subordinates, other managers, shareholders or the nation).

In the interview, one of the main problems is truth. No one listens seriously to an untrustworthy source of information. Therefore, if interviews are to function properly, those holding them must build up a reputation of trust.

Generally the conflict will be between the immediate interests of senior managers, and their long-term interest, or the long-term interest of the "management profession". It is easier to refuse people promotion, or a change of job, if you think their health will not be up to it and you send them for a medical examination. But it is not sincere, unless you are prepared to give them the job when they are cleared, if you don't tell them before they go that the job will not necessarily be theirs, even with a clean bill of health.

Applicants you are keen to recruit may easily get the impression, vaguely, that if they keep out of trouble they can reach the top.

The most compelling argument against the short-sighted deception is to have to hold the mopping-up interview afterwards.

On a wider scale, a manager may feel obliged, in the interests of shareholders and existing employees, to deny a rumour of redundancy. If the obligation is felt by managers to be one which always overrides the truth, then there ceases to be any point in giving the assurance. A denial is expected, whatever is to happen. It is no more trusted than a statesman who denies any intention to devalue the currency. If all managers put their priorities in this order, the whole profession of management gets a bad reputation and all suffer. The sad state of industrial relations is in part the result of this kind of mistrust.

The aim of an interview must be legitimate. It is not a legitimate aim (but it may be a legitimate means) to "take someone down a peg". It must be a fair balance of conflicting loyalties. If both parties to an interview can only implement policy, it is flattering, but in the long run frustrating, to pretend that the interview can create policy out of nothing.

5. Communication without words

Interviewers should appreciate the variety and value of non-verbal messages.

1. If not words, then what?
Silence
Pauses, hesitations, "er"s
Tone (upset or relaxed)
Pitch (soprano or bass)
Volume (loud or soft)
Speed
Grunts
Facial expression (eyes are the most effective communicators, in relation to the effort involved)
Head (nods) and hands (gestures)
Place (distance, angle of stance, behind a barrier)
Touch
Behaviour (offering a cigarette)
Appearance (dress; tidiness).

2. To convey what sort of message?
Conflict, worry and doubt ("I'm not sure of my facts")
Emotions (fear, anger, pleasure, embarrassment)
Attitudes (admiration, affection, dislike, impatience, loss of confidence, respect, surprise, etc)
Humour (amusement, cheerfulness)
Habits (personality, class, "image")

15

Appeals and threats
"You speak now".

3. Friendliness cues and control cues

In a meeting, many non-verbal cues can be analysed in two ways:
(a) indicating friendliness or warmth (or a desire for these), and
    the opposite, hostility
(b) indicating control and domination (or a desire for these), and
    the opposite, submissiveness.

The cues for friendliness are coming close, the angle formed between two people talking, smiles, eyes, tone of voice and sympathetic grunts. The cues for control are talking loud, fast and most of the time, in a confident manner, interrupting, controlling the topic, giving orders, ignoring feedback and relaxing.

Both these systems provide a framework for appeal and threat, reward and punishment, as ways of inducing "the other to do our will".

Friendliness and sympathy are rewards. Disagreement and frowns are punishments. Those exercising control can use their power to threaten or reward the submissive. The submissive can appeal to the other's superior power, where the satisfaction of granting the appeal is a reward, and the confession of failure implied by a refusal is distasteful.

4. Examples

The sample interviews on pages 22 to 26 illustrate, as far as a script can, many of these non-verbal exchanges.

6. Keeping control of the interview

The interviewer must adapt ways of controlling discussion to the topic or phase of the interview (giving or getting information, solving a problem or influencing attitudes). The chief variations in control are to be found in:

(a) the relative amount or talking done by each party
(b) the tempo of the interview
(c) the degree of freedom allowed to the interviewee

16

(d) the digressions allowed
(e) the emotional tension or relaxation.

For example, in the attitude-influencing interview, interviewers will generally do well to control the interview with a light hand and a loose rein by indirect methods, such as intermediate and final summaries, and the use of questions. They should realise that the most effective influence on attitudes and opinions will:

(a) come from interviewees stating the problem in their own words
(b) come from allowing them to overstate their case, and so see the weaknesses for themselves

rather than from trying to ram home views. Interviewers should maintain an impartial attitude; although they must (if and when appropriate) sincerely state their own views in an unprovocative and undogmatic manner.

7. Use of questions

The interviewer's main instruments are questions. The person asking the questions controls the interview, and so the interviewee should be checked from asking questions except at a stage in the interview set aside by the interviewer for the purpose.

Questions may be used:

(a) to encourage the interviewee to relax or to concentrate
(b) to draw out knowledge, experience, information, opinion
(c) to amplify and explain statements
(d) to keep the discussion relevant
(e) to bring out distinctions and similarities
(f) to reintroduce a point overlooked
(g) to encourage intelligent judgement
(h) to exercise discipline
(i) to check emotional thinking.

Questions should seldom be formed in a way which implies criticism or disagreement by the interviewer; such questions will not serve the purpose of the interview. Thus "Do you mean...or...?" should only be used if the interviewer has a genuine and explicable doubt; otherwise "If I understand you correctly, you are saying..." is better.

Questions are "open" if the length as well as the nature of the answer depends on the answerer, for instance "What would be the good and bad results of...?" They help the interviewer to assess the mood and personality of the interviewee, as well as to obtain information.

"Limiting" questions, or questions which are not open, are capable of being answered "Yes" or "No" or very briefly, with little scope for the answerer to influence the answer.

They are useful when the interviewer wants to avoid hesitancy or strain, as when starting an interview with someone shy; or for emphasising a vital point; or bringing an interview back on to the rails.

Who?
Where? } introduce limiting questions.
When?

Why?
How?   } introduce open questions.
What?

8. Difficult people and topics

Interviewees may be:

(a) over-talkative
(b) irrelevant
(c) impatient (wanting to jump to a decision)
(d) closed minds, a single point of view
(e) dogmatic, making unsupported statements
(f) duellers, more concerned with winning an argument than finding the best solution to the problem
(g) destructive and uncooperative
(h) inattentive; interrupting; or just not listening.

With such people interviewers should when possible depersonalise the matter away from themselves, often by questions which refer the interviewee back to the main objective:

18

"Do you feel we are making progress...?"
"Shall we agree to leave that point for the time being?"
"How does this point of view help us to reach a solution?"

Sometimes a restatement of the topic will bring an interview back on to the rails. In extreme cases, adjourn the interview.   Among difficult topics are points involving:

- criticism of higher authority
- comparisons unfavourable to the company
- disclosure of matters reflecting badly on the employee
- value-judgements of individuals or functions
- new practices which are contrary to a person's pet ideas.

Interviewers can agree to investigate a grievance against higher authority; but if they take sides with the interviewee against higher authority, they change their relationship with the interviewee, their own status, and the objective of the interview. Embarrassing or emotionally loaded comments should be drained of their emotional content, and discussion confined to those aspects which the interview can influence and improve.

An interviewer who is careful to remain impartial, objective, unemotional and sincere, and keeps in view the ultimate aims of the meeting, can usually resolve these difficulties.

9. Controlling the level of anxiety

The anxious are inhibited, and therefore cannot communicate effectively.

BUT: The over-confident, over-relaxed see no reason to discuss unpleasant matters; they have no motive for doing so; so they do not communicate effectively either.

SO: If the anxiety-level is too high, it should be lowered, and if it is too low, it should be increased.

To reduce anxiety
Convey:
    Desire for the interviewee to talk
    Trust

Undivided attention
No hurry

By:
Signs of affection or understanding
Reassurances
Relaxed conversation
Relaxing oneself
Distractions, digressions
The grunt sympathetic
Offering suggestions, taking care not to arouse resentment
Referring indirectly and metaphorically
Waiting for the interviewee to have the insight

To increase anxiety
Convey:
Serious nature of subject
Importance of the occasion
Authority of communicator
Urgency
Formal, cold relationships
Unpleasant consequences

By the opposite techniques to those for reducing anxiety, and especially:
Emotional withdrawal
Increasing distance, literally
Precise use of words

And if need be:
The sharp answer
Putting the interviewee in a difficulty
Enquiring about a matter known to be a cause of conflict

In the first sample interview (p. 22) the boss is reducing the level of anxiety; in the second (p. 24), increasing it.

10. Restatement

A good way to encourage the interviewee to continue explaining a point is to restate it, showing interest, and showing that you understand and sympathise in outline, but would like more detail. For example:

Statement: "She's not interested in helping me. In fact I think she's got something against me."
Restatement: "You think she's got a grudge against you?"
Statement: "Well, she's very unfriendly, and has been ever since last year."
Restatement: "Ever since last year, she's had a grudge?"
Statement: "Yes, well, I think so. You remember, the time we had to change the figures..." (See p. 23.)

The boss reflects or echoes what the subordinate has said.

A few points to note

- Do not restate so obviously or frequently as to disturb the flow of the interview. The last thing you want is for subordinates to imagine they have walked into an echo-chamber.

- Do not be a parrot: use your own words.

- Do not "read between the lines", or guess at something left unsaid.

- Allow plenty of time for a reply. The interviewee may be groping for words, and is best left to do this alone. If need be, restate the restatement. Do not let silence lead you to abandon that line of enquiry and start another.

- If you are repeating facts do not restate every detail, but sum up the main point or points.

- If you are restating attitudes or feelings, and the interviewee has mentioned several or expressed a point in several ways, restate the last one. Begin the restatement with some such phrase as "You feel that...", or "It seems to you that..."

- It is nearly always better not to indicate whether you agree or disagree with a statement, or whether or not you believe that an attitude is reasonable. The wish to reach agreement will give the incentive to produce more explanatory detail.

11. Redefining

Early in every interview the boss should define the problem with which the interview is to deal. But during the course of the interview, the nature of the problem may turn out to be different from the original definition. The boss should then redefine it.

One problem may turn out to be several. One aspect of a problem may be simple to solve, another may need to be deferred, another still may be insoluble.

A subordinate may bring a grievance which is in reality emotional as well as factual. The words state the facts and the tone indicates the emotions. The redefining may reduce or eliminate the emotional part, and concentrate on the facts. If there is personal hostility, this will be excluded from the redefinition. The boss then needs to get this redefinition accepted, with some such question as, "Is that right? Have I covered the main points of your complaint?" The subordinate will not normally reply: "No! The main point is that I hate your guts!"

Redefining is a special case of restating. It will sometimes serve as an intermediate summary, where the problem has taken a long time to analyse. Like the intermediate summary, it serves as a starting-off point for the next "paragraph" of the interview.

12. Sample interviews

1. Grievance

Pat Lowe (Boss): Come in, Sam. Just a second while I clear the air.
　　　(Clears a space on his desk)
　　　How are you? (Slowly looks up, sympathetically)
Sam Steel (Subordinate): (Furious) I've had just about enough of those typists. They spend half the day reading sloppy magazines and tarting themselves up, and when it comes to doing an honest piece of typing they get very rude. How can we do our work if they don't pull their weight? They say they're rushed, but whenever I go in, half of them are not working. That supervisor, Mrs Tattle — I'm sure she's to blame. (Stops for breath)

PL   Have you spoken to Mrs Tattle?

SS   Yes I have, but she just backs up the typists. You must speak to her. She'd have to listen to you.

PL   When did you speak to her? (Takes pencil and paper)

SS   I've just come from there. She said she can't promise to have my report on Spacklenuts ready for 10 days, and you know the Export Committee want to read it today week.

PL   Did you explain that?

SS   Yes, but she says she can't help that. She's not interested in helping me. In fact I think she's got something against me.

PL   You think she's got a grudge against you?

SS   Well, she's very unfriendly, and has been ever since last year.

PL   Ever since last year, she's had a grudge?

SS   (Slows down, looks away from Pat Lowe, shifts his feet, mumbles) Yes, well, I think so. You remember — the time we had to change the figures in the Product Analysis report — she made it pretty clear she blamed me for that.

PL   I see. (Leans closer) And you think she's still taking it out on you for that.

SS   Yes, I think so.

PL   Is there any other reason for her unkindness?

SS   (Grunt of contempt) I don't know. No justifiable reason.

PL   She hasn't any justifiable reason.

SS   Well, no, it's her petty regulations, with this form that she wants filled up with every report, saying who it's from, and how many copies on pink paper and all that guff — she's got no right to ask for that, but I do it to oblige her, and when I get the numbers in the wrong column she loves to take it out on me.

PL   How many reports have you sent her in the last month?

SS   About three, I suppose, some of them...

PL   (Interrupting) About three. Right. Have you filled up her form each time?

SS   Well, no. I filled it up once but the other times —

PL   Once you filled it up, twice you didn't. Was there any reason for that?

SS   It didn't seem necessary. Can she insist on that being completed? I tell them what I want.

PL   Yes, but if you were in her shoes, wouldn't you be glad to have typing instructions in writing?

SS   No — Well, it oughtn't to be necessary.

PL   Do you know anyone else who doesn't fill up the forms?

SS   No one likes filling them up.

PL   (Repeating the question) Do you know anyone else who doesn't fill them up?

SS   No, I don't.

PL   Are the typists as rude to everyone as they are to you?

SS   I don't know. (Pause) No, possibly not.

PL   Well, if you will try to fill up Mrs Tattle's form, I expect they will be polite. Come and see me next week. Are you free on Thursday at 10.30?

SS   Yes, I think so.

PL   ...And we'll see if the work is flowing a bit more smoothly.

2. Reprimand including preparation

PL   (Alone; thinking aloud) What am I to do about Sam Steel? I've got to get through to him somehow; to get him to fill up the typists' instructions and submit his reports to the typing pool in good time. Let's see. . . he's done how many reports? Where are they? This one on Marginal Output, this on the Effect of Tariffs; they were both very delayed; and this last one on the Cost/Productivity Ratio wasn't ready in time to be reviewed by the Export Committee. Yes, I've got the relevant dates; now what will he think? Blame the typists, very likely. Well, they can be difficult and overworked, but he must allow for that. Does he plan his work properly? Not very likely. He must be made to accept responsibility. I spoke to him on: when? (Looks in his diary) about these delays three weeks ago.

So far, then, I've got (Ticks off on his fingers)

   1. Previous record — poor
   2. Discussion three weeks ago
   3. No sign of improvement.

What sanctions have I got? I can't sack him. I can't demote him. I probably can't frighten him very much. So the negative sanctions are not helpful. What positive sanctions or rewards? Team spirit? What does he want to do? Perhaps there is some underlying problem. I'll have to see. Is there any action I could take? Closer supervision perhaps? Yes; I might get him to report his progress twice a week, and keep him up to the mark that way. Now let's set aside half an hour for this. Should be over in that time. I think tomorrow would be a good day. I can ask him what progress he's made on the Barium Draft.

Next day

PL   Come in.

SS   (Comes in) Hello Pat. What was it? (Sits in chair)

PL   Look — I've got something serious to talk about.

SS   Uh-huh.

PL   I've had enough of your casual approach. (Steel tenses up) I thought when I spoke three weeks ago on the subject of late reports, I would have no more trouble.

SS   Late reports? (He is playing for time)

PL   Yes, do you remember?

SS   Do you mean your complaining that the reports weren't ready in time, and that it was my fault?

PL   Yes, you do remember, then.

SS   But I told you. These typists, they sit on their chairs and knit, and every time I ring up and enquire how my draft is going they say they're very busy and haven't time to discuss it. I explained this to you.

PL   Yes, but did I accept your explanation?

SS   Well, I can't remember.

PL   Try. Do you remember anything I said?

SS   Well, you said you expected better things.

PL   Did I say that it would be all right if the typists continued to delay reports?

SS   No, of course not, but it's not my fault.

PL   Whose responsibility is it to get the draft ready on time?

SS   If the organisation doesn't provide enough typists...

PL   Is it the organisation's responsibility?

SS   Up to a point, yes.

PL   Could you make out a case for more typists?

SS   No, I haven't enough information.

PL   Well, it's your responsibility, and mine, to get the reports ready on time, or else explain properly why they're delayed. Agreed?

SS   Yes.

PL   For your next report I want a plan of how long it will take you, and how long you are allowing to type. I will discuss this with Mrs Tattle, the Senior Typist. And I need a progress report twice a week on whether we are up to schedule or behind schedule starting next Thursday at 10.30 am.

SS   I see. All right.

Chapter 2
The Selection Interview

1. Aims

1. To help in the process of choosing people for jobs by

   (a) informing applicants about the jobs
   (b) predicting which applicants will be able and willing to do the jobs
   (c) influencing suitable candidates to accept.

2. To show all the applicants, including the failures, that the organisation is a good one, and has tried to be fair. To create a good "image", or goodwill.

2. Drawbacks

In addition to the difficulties of conducting any interview, there are special difficulties with the selection interview.

1. Both sides know that much is at stake. The selection process is at least as important and as difficult as replacing a wrong selection. It is a tense interview.
2. The interview forces employer and applicant into acting. Employers present an impression of themselves and the job. Applicants present an impression of themselves and their ability and enthusiasm. Both may feel they have a vested interest in suppressing a part of the truth and exaggerating other parts. The winning applicant may be merely the one who is good at being interviewed.
3. The selection interview is unreliable, in that different interviewers assess the same candidate differently. The selection interview is a subjective way of reaching what ought to be an objective conclusion.

4. The task of predicting how applicants will perform seems difficult. Previous predictions may be known to have been mistaken. The longer term the prediction, the less valid it is likely to be, and often a selection interviewer has to make a prediction covering the rest of the working life of the applicant.
5. The "halo effect" is particularly dangerous. Even though we are not consciously prejudiced, it is almost impossible to avoid taking some reflex decisions when we first meet an applicant.

Interviewers need answers immediately to certain questions, such as What mood is the applicant in? What language is going to be suitable for the interview? before going any further. Our whole sensitivity to others depends on making continuous judgements of this kind quickly.

The danger is that this kind of first impression makes it difficult to answer the more important questions accurately. People who are neat, sunny and pause before speaking, may be automatically slotted in as hard-working, honest, good-tempered, creative and intelligent. Confidence tricksters rely on this human failing of judging the whole from only a sample, usually the first sample.

Conversely, the "cloven hoof effect" is assuming from dirty shoes, a coarse accent, scruffy clothes and a weak smile, that you have someone idle, ignorant and unreliable.

If the post calls for someone who makes a good first impression, an applicant who does not take the trouble to look presentable for the interview may be no good. It is still better to withhold judgement on these things until after the interview.

Point for thought: is there a reverse cloven hoof effect, in which you assume the applicant is a confidence trickster because the shoes shine too brightly, the agreement is too quick? No doubt. That must surely be just as bad.

3. What can be done outside the interview

The aims (see 1 above) include helping in the process of choosing people for jobs. This process will include much besides the actual interview:

1. Long-term organisation planning. Every manager should have, locked up in a drawer probably, a projected organisation chart

for five years ahead showing what staff will then be needed. No doubt, like real organisation charts, it will need continuous amendment, and will always be slightly out of date. Every selection should be compatible with the long-term plan. Is it necessary to recruit anyone at all?

2. Advertising. Consider the merit of internal promotion against outside recruitment.

3. The basic answers to the questions:

(a) What is the job?
(b) What kind of person am I looking for?
(c) How will I spot such a person?

These questions will be dealt with later in sections 4, 6, and 8: Job description, Personal profile, and Interview structure.

4. The statement of aims defined the ideal applicant as one who is able and willing. There are various more complicated ways of analysing qualities before selection: the Nine Point Plan, the Five Point Plan, and so on. This book will concentrate simply on the two points, able and willing, partly because they are easy to remember, and partly because they emphasise the distinction between those skills you can measure outside the interview, and that interest and enthusiasm for which the interview is important. For example, there are tests of:

(a) intelligence (verbal, numerical)
(b) health (medical examination)
(c) imagination (artistic, problem-solving)
(d) skill (manual dexterity, shorthand)

Film actors submit to screen tests and army officers to tests of initiative. Probably tests exist for the abilities that any interviewer would be able to define. The snag is that they take time to arrange and professional skill to interpret. It would be as dangerous for an amateur to run and interpret an intelligence test as for an amateur to conduct a medical examination.

5. There are other sources of information besides tests and the interview:

(a) qualifications (academic qualifications may replace intel-
    ligence tests)

29

(b) details of experience, supported by references (but see p. 35)

(c) the letter of application.

4. Job description

1. Title and context

Job title. Purpose. Grade. Location. Status. Number of employees in this job. Recognised trade unions. Place in the organisation. To whom responsible. For whom responsible. Closely related jobs. Date of job description, and date to be reviewed.

2. Pay and terms of contract

Pay. Basic, range, guaranteed minimum, sick pay, expected increments, piece rates, incentives, commission, productivity bonus, average earnings, overtime, superannuation, method of payment and of reviewing payment.

Expenses. Car, tools, clothes, travelling, accommodation, removal expenses, subsistence.

Fringe benefits. Pensions, canteen, discount goods.

Deductions. Union, social, welfare, savings schemes.

Terms of employment. Hours of work, holidays, period of probation, period of notice, procedures for dismissal and redundancy.

3. Duties

Sequence of operations. Standards of quality and output. Plan. Set output targets. Estimate the work content of jobs. Progress work. Methods. Use or be responsible for machines, repair or maintenance. Effort and skill needed. Average proficiency time. Creative work. Art, invention, problem solving. Beginning new projects.

Responsible for people. Interview, train, supervise, dismiss. Keep staff records. Control timekeeping and absence. Responsible for safety. Cooperate with union representatives. Committees. Speak in public or to meetings.

Sales. Receiving, telephoning, writing to customers or suppliers. Check stores. Chase supplies. Work with equals and superiors. Responsible for cash. Prepare budgets, keep accounts, compile

tables and graphs, write letters and reports.
Usual difficulties or causes of failure. Usual reasons for job satisfaction or job distaste.
Method of measuring work progress; job review or other way of telling job holder of progress.

4. Working environment

Ease of getting to and from work, parking or firm's transport; heat, cold, noise, dampness, on job.
Time, irregular or shift work, being "on call".
Special or protective clothes. Posture, physical comfort.
Work speed, variety, monotony, eyestrain, nervous strain, opportunity to rest and smoke. Social or solitary features of job. Element of danger. Health hazards.

5. Training and prospects

Eligibility for training. Time (full or part time), place (internal or external, on or off the job), and kind of training.
Opportunities for transfer, training and retraining. Criteria for transfer, training and promotion. Method of promotion.

5. Comments on the job description

This catalogue is no more than a check list which may help those preparing for a selection interview. Those who are close to a job can easily overlook some obvious elements if they do not check their description against such a list. Those who do not use a job description will hardly be able to assess which are the aspects to remember when it comes to interviewing.

Many of these points will be irrelevant to any one job. Other points will need elaboration. Some points will be essential, others desirable. In senior posts, the job description becomes what the holder makes it. The job description should clarify the job, but not fossilise it. Even if technical innovation did not require managers to revise job descriptions regularly, labour turnover would force them to do so. New staff with new attitudes, or even the same staff with developing experience, change the nature of the work they do.

It is logical to consider the job description before the kind of person we need to fill the job. But the process is two-way: jobs have to fit human beings, as well as human beings fit jobs. The growing and more civilised practice is to extend the control that individuals have over their work. This does not make the job description unnecessary, but perhaps chunks of it have to be marked "subject to negotiation".

Once in existence, the job description serves many purposes. It can help the organisation by highlighting (taken with other job descriptions) gaps or areas of conflicting overlap. It can help with work study, and studies of productivity, career development, pay structure, training needs and promotion.

The job description is tied to one job, but an individual is not necessarily recruited for only one job. Sometimes the employer needs someone to do two or more jobs in sequence, for instance in planning to replace someone due to retire soon. To find the right person it will be necessary to collect two or more job descriptions. Some firms recruit qualified staff (graduates, for instance) without knowing which actual job they will do. There is a danger in finding a person who is, in vague terms, employable at a certain level and salary, and then finding that none of the jobs actually available at that level fits the person's particular characteristics. The moral is that even recruitment to a certain grade covering a range of jobs should depend on job descriptions. It is not enough to say what qualities the successful applicant should have. It is not enough to say that these people must be transferable. These statements need to be related to the content of some or all of the alternative jobs, one of which the recruit will have to occupy.

6. The personal profile

1. Is X able?

(a) Physically
Weight, height, build, strength, stamina, hands, legs, eyesight, hearing, nerves
What physical handicaps would be acceptable?

How important is the first impression, good looks, physical coordination, way of standing, way of walking?

What physical activities at school would we expect to be relevant? What interests and hobbies would X have? What physical aspects of previous employment and experience would be relevant?

Is manual dexterity or mechanical dexterity important enough to be worth testing outside the interview?

Do we need a medical examination? If so what are the specific jobs for which the doctors need to pass X as medically fit?

(b) Mentally
Intelligence, knowledge, experience, skill, judgement
Original, creative faculty.
Critical, judicial faculty.

What academic qualifications do we expect? What interests and hobbies? What subjects and activities at school would X have been likely to do well?

Is intelligence an important enough factor to justify tests conducted by an appropriate specialist? Or would the academic record be a good enough guide to intelligence? What is the minimum acceptable level of intelligence? Is there a maximum?

What other skills would be better assessed by tests outside the interview? Numerical ability, oral ability, verbal skill; tests of creative imagination, or problem-solving ability; tests of concise writing?

What professional training and qualifications would be relevant? Should X be able to learn fast?

Should X have previous experience of similar work? What are the key areas where previous experience is vital? What should X have learnt from this experience? What skills should X have developed?

What organising ability does X need? Should X be able to organise other people's work?

What skills in dealing with people are needed? Carrying out orders, briefing subordinates, speaking in public, speaking in committee, interviewing, putting a case to a group?

How far must X conform to the attitudes and behaviour of the present team or organisation? How much divergence from the customs and behaviour of the present team would interfere with efficiency? How much would be a useful corrective to a stereotyped group with a narrow outlook?

Should X have any skills, knowledge or experience in reserve, over and above what the job may require?

2. Is X willing?

(a) Ambition
Do we want someone content to stay or ambitious to move? What ambitions of the individual would fit career prospects which the employer could offer?

What motives and "drives" would be most appropriate? Money, security and stability; change and variety; popularity; serving the community; travelling; job interest; self-development; independence.

See Appendix A on Equal Opportunities before you decide to consider whether the job would be more likely to suit a man or a woman, a married or a single person, someone with commitments (children, a mortgage) or someone without.

What scale of values would be appropriate? Should X be cautious or courageous, rigid or flexible, a rebel or a conformist? How much will X have to be trusted? How important is it that X be truthful; loyal to friends, to equals, to subordinates, to superiors; reliable; tactful?

What sort of subjects, hobbies and interests might X have enjoyed? For instance:

- artistic, creative, experimental, original
- social, organisational, in teams
- in public life
- do-it-yourself
- collecting and classifying
- commerical
- educational
- mental games, like cards or crosswords.

(b) Action
How hard will X have to push? How much energy does the job require? Could someone have too much energy to do the job satisfactorily? Those wanting a quiet person for a routine job

will have to identify and sift out applicants who need changes and challenges.

How much effort should X have put into work at school? Should the school achievement be greater than could be expected from someone of a given intelligence? Should X enjoy working hard to overcome obstacles? Should we expect interests or career events to show evidence of this?

Should X have worked beyond the duty laid down? Or developed the job? Are we looking for someone who meets failure with resignation, or bitter disappointment?

7. Comments on the personal profile

The personal profile is based on one or more job descriptions. I assume that the interviewer knows the job personally; it would hardly be possible to construct a useful personal profile from a job description alone.

The personal profile goes on to form the basis of the interview: of the tests, of the request for references, of other checks on the qualifications and experience of applicants.

The interviewer needs to predict how far applicants are able, and how far they are willing, to do the required job. It is convenient to divide the personal profile that way, notwithstanding the fact that the same piece of evidence will often prove relevant both to ability and to willingness.

There are valuable alternatives to the interview in assessing ability but hardly any alternatives in assessing willingness. In theory there are references. These depend on the attitude of the referees. No doubt an honest referee, with a good memory and the time to write a full reference and the courage to be candid, would give a useful reference. The interviewer would have to know the referee to be such. In certain professions, or inside one organisation, we may get near to these ideal conditions. In practice, an open reference is valueless; a confidential reference is limited by a referee's desire to help the applicant to reform or improve; a "present boss" reference is affected by the natural wish to hang on to the good and help the indifferent to move; a "past boss" reference is limited by how much the referee remembers, and how much the applicant has changed.

It is likely, therefore, that the greater part of the interview, and the more difficult part, will be concerned with the applicant's willingness. How much does X want to do the job successfully? How much energy will X bring to the task? This part of the personal profile is the most vital for the interviewer.

Do not think of a person merely as a collection of characteristics. One person is a unity which no other person ever fully grasps or can understand. Luckily we do not need to understand people fully in order to employ them effectively.

"I can tell what the applicant is like as soon as the door opens" is so arrogant and unscientific a statement that few openly make it. Yet we are all prone to put more value on immediate physical characteristics than they are worth. Red hair, blue eyes, brown skin provoke instant emotions, but they are irrelevant unless we are casting a play or running a strip club.

Racial discrimination is illegal (see Appendix B), but almost all forms of physical discrimination are antisocial. Disabled people are not unemployable, but their successful employment depends on finding them a suitable place. Be careful how you use the argument that "they would not be acceptable to other employees, or customers" as a reason for not employing applicants of a particular race or disability. This is the argument all prejudiced people use to indulge their prejudice while hiding behind the imagined prejudices of others. Give some thought to the effect of your decisions on the way society develops, and the reputation of "management".

Nearly all the ideal requirements are within a range from minimum to maximum. Avoid simply getting "the best person we can"; they may be too good for the job. There are limits on the amount of intelligence, knowledge, skill, ambition and energy that will fit a given job. Whales die in shallow water.

8. Interview structure

1. Beginning

Normally, applicants are nervous, and must be put at ease and be reassured of sympathetic treatment, or they will not talk freely and fully. The ways of reducing anxiety are described on p. 19

and are useful here. However, there are some other ways of reducing anxiety in a selection interview. Consider at the start offering a peppermint, a chocolate, a cup of tea or coffee, or even a glass of wine.

The interviewee should see something of the interviewer's own personality early on, perhaps by reference to some item of news, or a book on the desk, or some event earlier in the interviewer's day. This is to show humanity and to reduce tension; clearly it must be friendly, and gentle, or it may have the opposite effect. Slapping the applicant on the back does no good.

Then the subject may pass to neutral ground such as the journey and expenses. There is this to be said for asking applicants to submit expenses before the interview: they are more likely to be reasonable than later when they may feel the job is definitely theirs, or that they have absolutely no chance.

Next should come a few easy limiting questions. These are questions which the applicant should have no difficulty in answering; for an extreme example, "How many brothers and sisters have you got?" The more that nervous applicants can hear themselves answering confidently, the more their courage will grow.

Sometimes applicants are not nervous. They may not be interested in the job, in which case the sooner the fact is agreed the less time is wasted. But they may be first class, able to take their pick of jobs; the interviewer will be able to curtail these moves to relax the atmosphere, and give more time to the applicant's questions.

It seems unlikely that the interviewer would deliberately have to raise the level of anxiety at a selection interview.

2. Probes

Use the interview papers (the personal profile, the application form and references) to identify areas which would repay scrutiny. Do not ignore difficult or embarrassing areas, but leave them until the second half of the interview.

Most areas for probing can be dealt with according to a simple pattern. Start with a statement, either taken from the application form or from a previous statement of the interviewee. Follow this straight away with a limiting question. Listen to the answer. Then put an open question. By now the interviewee should have focused on the area you are looking at, and should give a long answer. When this answer is over, sum it up, emphasising any point you want to pursue. You can then repeat the pattern with another statement.

It might go as follows:

"You have put down stamp collecting as one of your interests. How many years have you been collecting stamps?"
"I started about 20 years ago."
"What is the appeal of stamps? Why do you collect them?"

Then you might get a long answer which you could sum up as:

"So what started as a simple hobby has become a useful source of income."

All the time you must keep control of the interview, be friendly and keep the level of anxiety down. If the applicant is longwinded, be prepared to interrupt one answer with another question. Keep an eye on the time. Do not let the applicant think the interview is a cross-examination; a check on the consistency of the applicant's answers should be either apologetic or subtle.

It will often be necessary to take notes during the interview. Take as few as possible, as it disturbs the flow, takes up time and raises the tension. Refer to the fact that you are taking notes, and apologise for it if you like. Do not take a note immediately after a mistake or after the applicant has been unable to answer a question; ask another easy question, and then make a note. Allow time to take notes immediately after the interview, which you will use when choosing the successful applicant.

3. The job
The applicant may reasonably expect to find out more about the vacancy during the interview. Much can be done before the interview, in the advertisement or in duplicated particulars sent to all the applicants. You could use either of these as the framework for talking about the job. You could use a copy of the job description, but this may contain too much information for an applicant to take in, or some information that you do not want to reveal to all the applicants.

There are two main purposes to this part of the selection interview. The first is to provoke questions for the next part of the interview. The second is to prevent the successful applicant saying, six months after accepting the job, "They never told me about this side of the work."

It is not difficult to provoke questions. It may be enough to describe what is obviously only half of one aspect, and say that you will be happy to answer any questions. The more difficult problem is how to prevent the successful applicant from feeling that the interviewer did not play fair, that some vital part of the work, or some intractable problem, has been kept secret. Plainly there is not enough time to discuss every aspects of the job in detail. The interviewer has to select what is important, and they may not agree on what things are important.

Moreover, most of us do change our tune according to how much we want the applicant. If we are beginning to think "not a strong candidate", we emphasise the unpleasant aspect of the job, to persuade the applicant to withdraw, or to make it easier to bear a rejection. There is not necessarily anything wrong in that. But the opposite, of telling the applicant we favour all the glamorous parts of the job, even exaggerating them, and playing down the unpleasant or problem parts, is unfair and unsafe. An applicant who is thus tricked into accepting the post, and slowly discovers the truth, will lose that trust and respect for the employer, or at least the interviewer, which is the basis of an effective working relationship.

For instance, it is dangerous to let someone gifted think all is set for rapid promotion, as a way of inducing that person to accept an inferior job. All parties to any discussion tend to remember the bits of the discussion that suit them, or excite them. They forget the parts that they want to forget. A selection interviewer may think that a few "ifs" and "buts", and some vagueness, will prevent trouble. But the applicant will probably imagine that the real vacancy being offered is a higher post than the advertised one.

4. Invite questions

This can be the most revealing part of the interview. Those who are about to commit themselves to a new job are making a more important move than an organisation that is about to commit itself to a new employee. They are surely entitled to discover at least as much about the job as the employer is entitled to find out about the applicant. They should get a chance during the office interview, and a chance during a walk around the workplace, which may be more fruitful.

The applicant's questions are revealing too: they tell the interviewer about the applicant's worries and hopes, experience and interests, and ignorance or insight into the job.

5. Ending

Efficient interviewers will end the interview when there are no more questions to ask and none to answer, or when the time is up, whichever is earlier. They must remember to give the applicants a feeling of having had a fair hearing from a good employer. The interviewer should thank them, and should make it clear what happens next, be it another interview, the payment of expenses or a letter giving the result of the interview. This should be automatic, and may sound perfunctory, like the opening sentences of the interview. But the end of the interview, like the beginning and the middle, must combine good manners with a feeling of direction and purpose.

9. Questions for selection interviewing

Preliminary chit-chat
1. Tea or coffee?
2. Did you have a good journey?
3. What were your travelling expenses?
4. How do you like living in ...?

Transition
5. What do you know about us? (Tell the candidate a bit more.)

Previous record
6. Did you like school?
7. What was your favourite subject? Why?
8. Did you decide to become a ... while you were at school?
9. Which of your jobs have you enjoyed most?
10. What was the best part of that job?
11. Did you get any valuable experience working with ...?
12. Are you glad you changed from ... to ...?

Personality
13. What are your main interests, apart from work?
14. What books have you read lately?
15. Where would you choose to live, ignoring the possibility of employment?
16. Who is your favourite character in history?
17. Do you think that TV has made people more illiterate?
18. What ambitions have you in work or social life? Do you see yourself in ... years' time in any particular job?

The vacancy
19. Had you any particular reason for applying for this job?
20. Do you mind ...? (Mention some of the drawbacks. Then describe the job.)
21. Is that fairly clear? Would you like to ask me any questions?

Geography
22. Have you thought about moving if you are appointed?
23. What are the advantages and disadvantages, geographically, of the move?
24. Can we help you with the move (loans, suggestions, etc)?

Conclusion
25. Thank you for the trouble you have taken.
26. We will be writing to you within ... days.

10. After the interview

1. Take notes on each applicant after each interview.
2. After all the interviews for one vacancy, ask yourself whether you have a number of applicants who would do the job well; or none who would do the job well; or one or two who would do it well, the rest being clearly less suitable.
3. If you have several who would be good, go through the job description and imagine each good applicant performing the various duties. You are looking for the person who has the best "extra" contribution to make.
4. If you have none who would do the job well, you have to decide whether to appoint no one or the applicant who is least unsatisfactory.

Go through the job description and imagine each applicant performing the various duties. Eliminate the ones who are so unsuitable that you would prefer not to appoint them. If there are any left, look for the one whose limitations would be the easiest to tolerate, or whose limitations could be most easily overcome by guidance, training, or redefining the scope of the job.

5. If one or two stand out, the selection process is relatively easy.

6. Remember the "long-term organisation plan" (see p. 28).

7. Keep some notes on the successful applicant for about six months. Then compare your verdict based on the interview with your verdict based on six months' work. This is a check on all parts of the selection process, but especially the interview.

8. Write to the applicants, and do whatever else you agreed at the interview to do.

9. Send a contract of employment to the successful applicant.

10. Arrange an induction interview for the first working day.

11. The panel interview

In many organisations, particularly large ones, the selection interview is conducted not by one person but by a panel of three or four (though I have heard of much larger panels). One of the panel is in the chair. Usually one is concerned with the job directly, whose task is to ask the technical questions. One is concerned with personnel policy: pay, holidays, training and so forth.

The advantages of a panel interview are:

1. A panel emphasises the importance and seriousness of the occasion. This should mean that the interviewers put more thought and effort into the interview.

2. The members of the panel can correct each other; if one mishears or misunderstands what the applicant says, the other can give their version.

3. The important responsibility for interviewing and selecting is shared. If the selection is successful, all can take credit. If it proves unsuccessful, no one person can be singled out as blameworthy. It is worth noticing that organisations which are accustomed to collective responsibility, and to taking important decisions in committee (the Civil Service, local government, academic bodies), favour the panel;

industry, which is used to executives taking individual responsibility, usually has one-to-one interviews.

4. The panel may obtain some advantage from the division of labour. Each member of the panel can specialise in one aspect, and may be able to ask better questions, and give better answers when the applicant asks, than any one person who has to deal with the whole field.

5. The senior member, usually the one taking the chair, can try to ensure that members of the panel have done their homework on the applications before the interview.

12. Disadvantages of the panel interview

1. Cost. If the panel has four members, one hour of interviewing costs four (probably expensive) working hours of interviewers' time.

2. The panel arrangement is inflexible in various ways. The time of the interview has to suit more people. If the time is fixed, the most suitable people may not be available. It may be impossible, or difficult, to get the same panel to meet again the next day; so panels are more likely than individuals to select a candidate on the same day as the interview, which restricts the opportunity to think it over.

If one member of the panel, or one applicant, is late or does not come, the time of more people is wasted. If the short-listed applicants are all to be interviewed in sequence by the same panel, they will have to wait nervously together in some waiting-room until they are called. And if the panel intend to offer the job the same day, they will have to wait nervously together after the interview as well.

3. It is more difficult to put the applicants at ease when they are so obviously outnumbered. The panel can all keep their eyes on one applicant at once; the applicant can only watch one of them at a time. If the panel all sit on one side of a table, and the applicant sits on the other side, the proceedings resemble an inquisition.

4. The art of chairing is as difficult as the art of interviewing. For instance, unless someone is strictly watching the time, it may be unfairly allocated among the panel members, or one dominating person may hog all the questions. On the other hand, if the interview keeps rigidly to an agreed programme, panel members may find

that they cannot pursue an interesting point because it is time to bring in someone else.

5. Each member of the panel thinks about the other members when asking questions, and not just about the job or the applicant. They are tense, because they do not want to say anything that the rest of the panel might think foolish. They may be inclined to show off by using sophisticated terms or talking about their own work. Some panels have to spend the first ten minutes putting themselves at ease, before they put the applicant at ease. The more people there are the longer it takes to find a "wavelength" in common.

13. Interviews in series

It may be possible to give the applicant a series of one-to-one interviews, with different interviewers, one after the other. It will take more of the applicant's time, but probably not significantly more in proportion to the total time they have given up to attend. It is likely to be more fruitful in proportion to the interviewers' time. In fact it has most of the advantages of the panel interview, while avoiding most of the disadvantages.

Chapter 3
The Interview at Work

1. The induction interview

After the embarrassment of selection, when the applicant was trying to do well, comes the offer and acceptance of a job. From then on, the applicant can (relatively anyway) relax. The first important interview in this state will probably be with the new boss. I call this the induction interview.

Large firms have induction courses. These are an excellent way of telling numbers of recruits the broad facts about their new place of work. It is an induction into the firm; as well as this, the recruit needs an induction into the actual job.

This interview is the foundation-stone of a sound relationship between subordinate and boss. It is used by each to find the other's wavelength. It is true that both may have met and talked during the selection process; but exchanges then need to be extended and confirmed now that their new relationship has begun.

The induction interview may overlap with an instruction or counselling interview. The manager will find it pays to take the interview slowly and seriously; the new recruit will be able to make a useful contribution sooner.

But try to remember what the first day in a new job was like for you. The interviewer finds it easy to go on talking, but you do not take in much. Ideally, the manager should fill in some of the background, and leave most of the time for the recruit to ask questions.

Aims
1. To help a recruit to fit in with a new working group
2. To get to know the recruit
3. To sort out any problems
4. To give the recruit confidence

5. To give job instructions.

Preparation
1. Plan the whole of the first day, if possible, before planning the interview
2. Investigate the interviewee; consult previous interviewers and correspondence
3. Plan the locations and timing; so long in an office, so long walking round the site
4. See that those to whom the recruit should be introduced are available
5. Ensure privacy for the office part of the interview.

Structure
1. Congratulate and welcome
2. Ask if there are any problems
3. Explain the day's programme and purpose
4. The job (Is there a written job description?)
5. The people
6. The amenities
7. The local customs
8. Sum up
9. Any questions?

Check results
1. Does the employee seem contented?
2. Is the work going well?
3. Are there any problems with "fitting in"?
4. Did the interview suggest that the recruit needed "watching" or guidance on any special point? Was it in fact needed? Has it been given?
5. Make a further chance to ask questions at a follow-up interview.

2. The grievance interview

Those in authority do not usually welcome grievances. We all have defensive emotional reactions which are basic and strong, and which lead us instinctively to deny a criticism instead of turning it to our own advantage. In some emergencies, a critic of authority does more harm than good, but normally a grievance is valuable feedback that something has gone wrong. We should overcome our instincts, and thank the person who brings a grievance. If it is not a justified one, the manager can take the chance to put the illusion straight.

The manifest or declared grievance may not be the extant or real grievance. The manager would be wise not to dismiss someone's grievance simply because it is plainly false. First try to establish the real grievance. There is a tradition that complaints about canteen food signify poor morale or worsening industrial relations. Strikes over wage differentials occur less because of the actual money involved, which is often little enough, than because of what the differentials symbolise: status.

Someone who has a private worry and is unsure whether to discuss it with the manager, may use an artificial grievance as a way of securing the manager's attention. The manager should use questioning, restating and redefining techniques carefully, in a friendly and encouraging way, to turn a bogus grievance interview into a genuine counselling interview. The initiative in this interview rests with the person with a grievance. The manager should therefore cultivate the habit of doing the "preparation" in the first minutes of a spontaneous grievance interview.

Remember that those who are angry can be calmed more easily by action or planned action than by apologies. And counter-criticism is, emotionally at least, counter-productive.

Aims
1. To end the grievance and so improve morale
2. If the grievance is justified, to remove the cause and so improve efficiency.

Preparation
1. Take time to investigate, if possible
2. Clarify your own rights and powers, and what the organisation's policy is
3. Ensure privacy.

47

Structure
1. Welcome the grievance
2. Listen to the grievance
3. Restate it in your own words
4. Get assent to your restatement
5. Give your own interpretation of the facts
6. Say what you have done so far
7. Say what you intend to do, but do not limit your freedom to manoeuvre if something unexpected occurs
8. Give reasons for your interpretation and action
9. End on a note of appreciation and sympathy.

Check results
1. Check morale
2. Check that the grievance has ended, and no substitute grievance has arisen
3. Check relations and attitude
4. Check performance and efficiency.

3. The instruction interview

Using the interview to instruct is common enough, particularly among staff whose work normally includes interviews for other purposes. It is perhaps not normally considered as one of the kinds of interview, because instruction is traditionally either "sitting next to Nellie" or else something that goes on in a classroom.

Nevertheless the interview is a concentrated and effective kind of instruction. It corresponds to private tuition. It is ideal for individuals who do not want their ignorance exposed to a class. It is necessary when only one person needs the lesson. It may be the only way to put across something that depends on individual reactions: how to handle a difficult subordinate, or how to put a case to a committee or customer.

The instruction interview can arise from the progress interview. It is closely related to the correction interview.

Aims
1. To get a job done well and willingly

2. To draw out the abilities of the individual.

Preparation
1. Establish the extent of the job
2. Consider how the job fits into the work of the whole organisation
3. Consider how the job fits into the career and development of the individual
4. Prepare examples for demonstration or other visual aids
5. Consider the points that most need emphasis
6. Plan the instruction; make notes
7. Establish when the instruction will be carried out
8. Decide how closely performance should be supervised.

Structure
1. State purpose of the interview
2. State how the job fits into the work of the whole organisation
3. Define the job; demonstrate if possible
4. Invite questions and answer them
5. Recapitulate the difficult or important points
6. Express confidence in ability to perform it.

Check results
1. Check performance of job
2. If done well, congratulate; if not, consider correction or reprimand.

4. The correction interview

I have distinguished between the correction and the reprimand, as these two types of interview need different treatment. To receive a reprimand, individuals must be clearly blameworthy; if they have done wrong but it is not their fault, because (for instance) they have been badly trained, the interview should be a correction.

A person who makes a mistake has a tendency to confuse the correction and the reprimand. First the wrongdoer is annoyed at the error, and its discovery, even (perhaps especially) if it is someone else's fault. It can be difficult to put somebody right without appearing to criticise. If innocent and sensitive people detect the least sign of unjustified criticism, they may "counter-attack" sharply, or alternatively nurse a grudge, according to temperament. They have interpreted a correction as a reprimand. On the other hand, someone receiving a reprimand has a vested interest in interpreting it as a correction. They may have done something incorrectly, but if it was someone else's fault, pride is not wounded.

The interviewer must sort out both sorts of confusion.

Aims
1. To improve performance
2. To prevent repetition
3. To protect others from carelessness or danger.

Preparation
1. Remember that, unlike a reprimand, the individual is not to be blamed
2. Take time to investigate, if possible, and see where the blame lies. If it is partly your own fault, admit it briefly
3. Take action outside the interview to prevent repetition of the mistake
4. Correct rather than reprimand for:
   (a) trivial errors
   (b) first offences without grave consequences
   (c) individuals in a new job or procedure; old habits may be asserting themselves, they may have been badly instructed or not have had enough experience
5. Plan the correction as a piece of training.

Structure
1. Point out the error
2. State that no blame is attached. Take the blame yourself if you can do so sincerely; be brief
3. Explain the effects of the error
4. Demonstrate the correct method in a way suitable to the individual
5. Ask questions
6. Make sure the correction is understood and accepted

7. Encourage self-correction.

Check results
1. See mistake is not made again
2. If it is, consider reprimading; if it is not, congratulate
3. Give the corrected person an opportunity to ask questions which he or she thought of after the correction was over.

5. The reprimand interview

The aims of the reprimand are the same as the aims of the correction. The aim is not to punish (though that may be a way of achieving the aim), nor is it to pass moral judgement; these are at best means. And the only effective means is for the culprits to reprimand themselves, to convict themselves. If they do not plead guilty, the interview becomes a fruitless conflict.

This interview is the manager's most difficult and unpleasant task. It can be a severe strain on the loyalty which everyone feels for their colleagues. But it is part of the manager's job. A boss who cannot reprimand is as useless as one who cannot give orders. The first point for the manager to grasp is that it is part of the work; that it will cut across social relationships; that loyalty to the firm must sometimes outweigh loyalty to a friend. The second point is that he must develop the skill required.

The reprimand is charged with emotion. Yet here, above all, those in authority must not lose their temper. In a reprimand there is no room for heated argument, only for a cold, realistic statement of disagreeable facts.

Aims
1. To improve performance
2. To prevent repetition
3. To protect others from carelessness or danger.

Preparation
1. Be sure of your ground
2. Take time to investigate, including the person's previous record
3. Plan reprimand in relation to the individual
4. Reprimand in private, subject to the next point

5. Consider bringing in your personnel department, and the person's trade union.

Structure
1. Get to the point at once
2. Get agreement on the facts; be exact
3. Get admission of the offence
4. Do not argue
5. Give a chance to reply fully
6. See that they understand the consequences of their behaviour
    (a) to their colleagues (the reasons behind the rules)
    (b) to themselves (disciplinary sanctions)
    (c) to their ideal of themselves (self-esteem)
7. Show them how to improve and show confidence in their ability to do so.

Check results
1. See error does not recur
2. Do not show antagonism
3. Check attitude and relationships
4. Check work generally.

6. The counselling interview

Sometimes a manager must be a social worker. By a counselling interview, I mean something which goes outside the normal working relationship between manager and subordinate. Organisations are made up of human beings, who bring to work not only their hands and their brains but also their private worries.

(Some people use "counselling" to mean a mild rebuke or a friendly warning, an alternative to discipline or appraisal, or part of those processes, initiated by the boss and directly related to performance. It is almost the opposite of the supportive, non-judgemental listening called "counselling" by social workers and the Samaritans. Those who use the word to mean managerial advice will need another word to describe the manager's social work interview.)

Employees in the grip of problems such as drugs or debt are seldom able to see the way out. They need help from someone they trust, who can see the problem dispassionately. Sometimes the manager can solve the problem and lay it on the table, pat. Sometimes it is enough to know who can help, or to be a sympathetic audience, while the subordinate thinks out loud, and so works through the problem.

In this interview, the manager's authority comes not from the status which the organisation bestows, but from the trust of the subordinate. If the manager abuses this trust, the working relationship will suffer, just as, until the problem is solved, the subordinate's work will suffer.

Difficult cases can waste a lot of managerial time. Bosses need the skill to reserve time and energy for their own job, without being unfriendly or brusque to someone less fortunate than themselves. Large firms, recognising the dilemma, have welfare officers to deal with such cases. But whether or not there is a welfare officer, the manager must learn some counselling skills.

Here are a few guiding principles:

1. Those who confide their private life to others expect secrecy and have a right to it. Tell no one about the discussion without permission, unless there is some higher moral principle involved.

2. Let them tell their own story; do not put words in their mouth.

3. If you must advise, put it in the form of a question: "Have you thought of going to the Citizens' Advice Bureau?"

Aims

1. To help employees solve their problems concerning work or their private life

2. To improve performance and working relationships by helping to solve these problems.

Preparation

1. If possible, set aside enough time so that the interview does not have to be cut short

2. Ensure privacy

3. Consider the person's background (education, home, work) and what problems you are expecting, if any

4. Consider what other persons or agencies (medical, social, legal, etc) might help

5. Consider how the team would cope with the work if you had to grant leave of absence.

Structure
1. Welcome and put at ease
2. The employee states the problem
3. Redefine the problem, analysing it into different problems where necessary
4. Take each problem separately; use short questions to open out the problem
5. Listen sympathetically
6. Contribute your knowledge of the persons or agencies available for help
7. Help to formulate a plan of action
8. Assure the employee of your help, and that these matters will be kept secret
9. Arrange a follow-up interview.

Check results
Hold any follow-up interview. This time five minutes may be enough.

7. The termination interview

A person who resigns from a job is well able to give constructive feedback about the organisation. There is no fear of reprisals, and so comments can be frank in a way that is hardly possible to those in continuing employment.

A good manager will not neglect this opportunity. Many firms collect "Reasons for Leaving" on a form, which every leaver completes, and the reasons are later slotted into categories and are presented as a table of statistics at the end of the year. But these reasons are at best superficial. An interview will get much closer to the truth than a form.

Finding out the background reasons for the resignation is part of the purpose of a termination interview, so that similar resignations can be made less likely in future. But it is only part. Even those who have a very obvious reason (promotion to a better job than they could obtain by staying put, or a spouse who wants to move out of the area) are worth interviewing. It may be that the firm is recruiting people too well qualified or too ambitious for the job. Those who are content in their move will make the more constructive and less embittered comments.

Where there is some bitterness, it may help if the termination interview is not conducted by the leaver's immediate boss. Some organisations arrange for a personnel officer to interview leavers; sometimes a manager other than the immediate boss may do it. Where the firm chooses to make a determined effort to persuade someone to withdraw a resignation, two or three interviews may be needed; and several interviews may be helpful in obtaining information even where there is no hope of keeping the person.

This interview would hardly be appropriate for someone who had been dismissed.

Aims
1. To improve the efficiency of the selection process
2. To remedy any organisation problems
3. To reduce staff turnover
4. To persuade the leaver to withdraw the resignation if appropriate
5. To improve the image of the organisation in the leaver's mind.

Preparation
1. Study the history of the leaver
2. Consider recent performance and behaviour for clues to reasons for leaving
3. Speak to the leaver's supervisor
4. Consider what you know of the leaver's home background.

Structure
1. Welcome and put at ease
2. Express regret at resignation
3. State purpose of interview
4. Ask reasons for leaving and general comments
5. Restate points and get assent to restatement
6. Correct any errors of fact
7. Make notes of serious points
8. Indicate what you will do towards preventing a recurrence
9. Offer thanks and good wishes.

Check results
1. Revise the job description and the personal profile for the leaver's job if necessary

2. Act on the points made in the interview
3. Check morale of those in similar jobs
4. Check staff turnover
5. Keep in touch with the leaver for six months.

Chapter 4
The Progress Interview

1. What is a progress interview?

Whenever a boss and a subordinate meet, just the two of them, to discuss how the subordinate is making progress, we have the kernel of a progress interview.

This is the most complex and difficult kind of interview to conduct. It calls for all the skills required at the other types of interview. It is usually made up of different strands, serving different purposes, combined in one interview. We discuss here the different strands, but this is not to suggest that it is possible to combine them all in one interview. Which strands are separated into different interviews, and which are combined, will depend on particular circumstances.

If the interview is not to be a pointless embarrassment, the interviewer must have a clear idea of its purpose, and of the dangers.

2. Aims of the progress interview

These aims can include one or more of the following:

1. To improve individual performance by knowledge of results
2. To reconcile the employee's ambitions with the employer's objectives
3. To improve communication between boss and subordinate
4. To help an individual to see and overcome failings
5. To help the manager to take stock of the subordinate's work
6. To help the manager to see and overcome any managerial or organisation failings
7. To help the subordinate to develop any talents
8. To give recognition of good work
9. To prevent the recurrence of old difficulties

10. To help the employer with recruitment planning
11. To identify outstanding staff early in their career
12. To assist the employer's salary administration
13. To help with the employer's redundancy or dismissal procedure
14. To plan future work and set targets or objectives.

3. Drawbacks of the progress interview

1. Boss and subordinate are frightened of changing their previous relationship.
2. In particular, boss and subordinate usually have a friendly social relationship, in addition to their working relationship. How do you joke with someone on one day and the next day bring bad news about promotion? How do you preserve the boss-subordinate relationship, without jeopardising the other happier, and more equal, relationship?
3. If there is some grievance or conflict between the two, smouldering beneath the surface, this interview may cause it to explode, hurting both without resolving the cause.
4. Reserved people, as the English often are, only talk about important things with difficulty and embarrassment.
5. The subordinate may be more quick-witted at interviews than the boss. This frightens the boss and may frustrate the purpose of the interview.
6. Where the boss judges the subordinate, the judgement will be subjective. The "halo effect" (see p. 28) applies to progress as well as selection.
7. The truth may be merely depressing. For instance, to tell someone that their hopes of advancement have been groundless may cause morale and performance to suffer rather than improve.

4. How not to do it

In some organisations, the subordinates look forward to their progress interview keenly, but their managers are shy of it.

The subordinate may spend days, or even weeks, anticipating the interview; fearing it perhaps; working out carefully every word to say; thinking about the year's work and conduct; framing questions to ask.

The boss also fears the interview, but it is more difficult to say why. Little preparation is done. The interview is held at Christmas, when it can be linked to an annual salary review, and to "tidings of comfort and joy". With a skilful secretary a boss tries to get through ten or more interviews a day, on top of the normal work.

It is tragic that all the subordinate's concentration and energy, and all the potential for discussion, support, recognition and improvement, which could benefit both the individual and the employer, should be wasted.

5. Progress or appraisal?

The word "appraisal" is commonly used to describe this interview, but it seems to me to be open to an important objection. It puts the emphasis on "evaluating" the subordinate, and evaluation is not an important part of the purpose. It may well not help towards achieving any of the purposes. If it is interpreted literally, it dehumanises the relations between interviewer and interviewee.

The *Shorter Oxford Dictionary* defines the words as follows:

Progress. A dozen meanings, including "advance, advancement; growth, development; usu. in good sense, continuous improvement".
Appraisal. "The act of appraising; the setting of a price".
Appraise. "1. To fix a price for; esp. as an official valuer.
2. To estimate the amount, or worth of."

Human beings do not want to be priced like second-hand cars. Managers do not want to be "official valuers".

An interview would not be necessary for that purpose at all. The object of the interview is the growth and development it encourages, and the name of the interview ought to emphasise this aspect.

The word "appraisal" reinforces the myth that people can be marked like examination papers, and that the total mark is all that matters. A "good" employee becomes one with a high mark, and the human race can be strung out along a one-dimensional spectrum. The mark relates to earnings. Managers become entitled to "judge" or "appraise" subordinates because they have more marks and larger salaries. Everyone works (the theory says) for more money or promotion, which terms become synonymous. The person with the highest mark of all becomes Prime Minister.

If this is ridiculous, why do so many "appraisal" schemes seem to be based on this kind of theory?

Many companies, and the Civil Service, have some assessment form or report about their staff, connected to their promotion policy, their manpower planning and career development. When they decide (as is commonly the case) to impose an appraisal or progress interview on all their managers, it is linked to this form or report. For administrative simplicity, managers have to tick boxes beside various qualities, each box representing comments or evaluations such as "outstanding", "average" or "unsatisfactory". Managers have to be "official valuers". And because the forms are used for a wide range of people in a wide range of jobs, the qualities tend to be vague: "Technical understanding", "A good influence" or "Shows initiative".

These forms may then be used to plan the career development of individuals. At this point another snag arises. If the "official valuers" know that the evaluation will be used like this, and affect a career, they change their attitude to the form, and indeed change the values, just as commercial valuers will give a minimum value for probate and a maximum for insurance.

Plainly we need at least two valuations, one for the administrative appraisal and another for the progress interview. If the administrative system, or the interview, concerns itself with the chances of promotion or transfer, we need a further subdivision. The value of a member of staff in their present job does not necessarily relate to their value in another job. An average clerk might become a first class supervisor. Equally we do not take our best surgeons and reward them for their excellent surgery by taking them away from the operating table and inviting them to administer a chain of hospitals. Industry does sometimes make this kind of mistake, and unless the system guards against the tendency, it will be likely to imply that all outstanding performers ought to be promoted.

What right, anyway, has the manager to make this appraisal? Do employers select managers because they are good judges of others, good appraisers? Their valuation will reflect their own temperament. Personnel departments which collate these valuations know that they tell you as much about the appraiser as the appraised. No doubt if all a manager's geese are swans (or vice versa) the system will spot it and make the necessary correction. Less easy to identify is the effect of personal sympathy or antagonism between a manager and one particular subordinate.

And if, in the interview, the manager communicates an evaluation or appraisal to the subordinate, how will it help the subordinate to develop or grow? The subordinate may agree with the appraisal. If the appraisal is critical, this could lead to despair, and if the appraisal is flattering, to complacency. A subordinate who disagrees is unlikely to benefit from the appraisal. The possible consequences include open conflict, a silent grudge and loss of confidence in the appraiser.

There is more sense in the idea that people in jobs are pegs of odd shapes in holes of odd sizes. "Progress" does not mean putting a peg into a bigger hole; at least, not necessarily. It is much more a case of finding a peg and a hole that nearly fit; of moulding the pegs (or, as they are human, enabling and encouraging them to mould themselves) to fit in the holes they prefer; and adapting the holes to fit the pegs. This is more complicated and difficult than just "the setting of a price", but it is also more rewarding.

The job of the progress interview is in many ways like the job of the selection interview. We saw there that it made little sense to look for the "best" recruit, and it was necessary to fit the person to the job. Let us abandon the idea of marking people or setting a price on them. The interviewer, the boss, is the representative of the employer at the progress interview. Employers should concern themselves with finding work which suits their staff, which uses their capacity to the full, and which extends the amount of their job that they enjoy and do well.

6. Boss-based or subordinate-based?

Imagine a progress interview which is entirely boss-based: the whole contribution and control comes from the boss. The boss completes a company assessment form, stating the qualities and shortcomings of the subordinate, and summons the subordinate to the managerial office. The boss passes on as much of the assessment as is good for the subordinate to know. If in the boss's view it is necessary or will help, the interview refers to possible salary increases or promotion, or to transfer or dismissal. The verdict may be supported by boss-selected evidence to indicate how the subordinate's performance compares with the targets and expectations of the boss. The boss sets targets and objectives for the future.

Now consider a subordinate-based interview. First, if the subordinate does not want an interview, there is none. The subordinate may devise an assessment form and complete it. The subordinate marks achievements and setbacks against targets which were self-imposed. Where those targets were not reached, it is the subordinate who gives reasons, suggests ways of overcoming difficulties, and asks for training or other support from the boss or employer. It is the subordinate who chooses the time and place (perhaps the usual workplace) of the interview. At the interview the boss reads or listens to all this. The subordinate asks for transfer or promotion, or may threaten resignation. The subordinate sets targets for the future.

Both these caricatures have their justification. The first resembles a law court, the second a confessional. As in a court, the first interview holds the subordinate captive. As the judge represents society, so the boss represents the organisation. In the second interview, the initiative rests with the person being judged, as in the confessional. The courts can use external pressure to force a person to conform; the confessional changes people from within. But these analogies must not be pressed too far. Managers have no prison. The most powerful sanction they have is probably people's self-esteem or vanity. But managers have a duty to protect the interests of the organisation, and they should be better able to "judge" what needs doing, and how to do it, than a subordinate. So there may be a time and a place for either of these two methods.

Usually the important thing is to get agreement between parties. Without this progress is hardly possible. Neither the boss-based interview nor the subordinate-based interview adequately allows for this. Where the boss is dealing with young or inexperienced subordinates, the boss-based interview may be nearer the mark. Where both parties are mature and cooperative, the subordinate may draw up the agenda and do most of the talking. Probably the ideal is some half-way house between the two extremes.

7. Short-term reviews

In some jobs work is easily measured and close control and feedback are important; in sales or production, for instance. For this purpose the team meet their manager regularly. These regular meetings are sometimes called "team briefings" or "briefing groups", which emphasises that the boss is informing subordinates of future plans. But future plans are also a function of the progress interview, and team briefings can include on a group level most of the other facets of progress interviews. Where the work suggests individual progress interviews rather than team meetings, the aims and content of such interviews will resemble the aims and content of "team briefings".

These short-term progress interviews may be held monthly, weekly or even daily. They aim to improve performance by analysing progress since the last interview. The existence of the interview is itself an incentive to the subordinate. Where progress is not satisfactory, both boss and subordinate are responsible for remedying it, and may best do this by discussion.

Among the subjects covered will be:

1. Progress since last interview
2. Any necessary remedial action
3. Decisions by higher management which affect the work of the subordinate
4. Targets to be achieved before the next interview
5. Any questions or suggestions.

One approach is to have meetings or interviews of this kind frequently but not regularly. Instead of having a "Monday morning prayer meeting" or a "First Tuesday in the month" type of fixture, they only hold a meeting when there is a specific item to discuss. They may have two interviews in one week, and then none for a month.

Although such irregular interviews may be supposed to save time, they have disadvantages. Most of us, when we get a message that the boss wants to see us, think instinctively "What have I done wrong now?", try to guess what the accusation will be, and prepare our excuses. If the interview was expected, we would come to it in a less defensive, and more receptive, frame of mind. And subordinates will be able to save up less urgent grievances for the expected interview, when they will put them with more care, and less emotionally, than if they had to raise them unexpectedly.

If the frequency is correctly established (daily, weekly or monthly) there will always be some of the subjects suggested above which will be worth discussing. It is up to the boss to see that the time is not wasted discussing something that would not be discussed, and that no one would want to discuss, were it not for the interview.

These short-term progress interviews are not usually imposed on a manager by the organisation. They are up to the individual manager and local circumstances. In this respect they are rather different from the long-term interview.

8. Long-term reviews

Much that we have said about short-term reviews applies equally to long-term. They should be regular and expected; they should include in principle what the short-term interviews include. But as they are held at longer intervals, annually or every six months, perhaps they have a different character. They tend to be more elaborate, they discuss more fundamental things, and they focus on the progress and career of the individual. This all makes them more difficult to handle.

If a boss holds both short-term and long-term interviews, the long-term interview will start from the base of the short-term interviews held in between. It will be a kind of consolidation.

If the annual interview is held without any short-term progress interviews in between, clearly it will need more thorough preparation.

Some long-term interviews are imposed by an employer throughout the organisation in an attempt to remedy bad management. If staff work for years without ever being told whether they are doing a good or bad job, their morale and efficiency will suffer. People have as much need of, and more right to, recognition, servicing and repair, as the machines they operate. But the right kind of interview is not necessarily the same across the board. There has to be a compromise between forcing all managers into a centrally designed strait-jacket which will make a number of people most uncomfortable, and on the other hand giving managers so much room for manoeuvre that some avoid serious interviews with subordinates altogether.

This needs tackling from a number of different directions at once. Training, starting progress interviews at the top and working down, writing the job descriptions of senior managers so as to include some progress interviewing, and a gentle analysis of the more difficult areas, can all contribute to a solution.

9. Job objectives

Employees are entitled to know what standard of work is expected of them. One purpose of having a written set of job objectives for each job is simply to tell them that standard.

The second, related purpose is to prevent the progress interview, and other interviews, from being merely an exchange of impressions and opinions. A good worker is one who gets good results; not the one with an attractive personality or an aggressive voice, unless these go with good results.

Job objectives should be based on the job description (see p. 30). They should highlight those duties which contribute most to success or failure. Against each duty should be given a standard of quantity or quality. A typist might have a job objective giving the number of pages, or square inches, of typing an hour, and a maximum number of complaints or errors a week.

Job objectives, whether of quantity or quality (and the two overlap), should as far as possible be matters of fact, admitting no dispute. If the objectives have to be matters of judgement, the judge should be someone other than the boss or subordinate.

Those who are accustomed to vague qualities of the kind sometimes mentioned on assessment forms, such as "initiative", "good judgement" and "communication skill", will not see how to translate these into job objectives. Indeed, as long as they remain simply abstract words which one person attributes to another, it cannot be done.

If employees are employed and paid simply for characteristics they possess, and not for any work they might do, there is no place for job objectives, or for progress interviews either. And no doubt there are such people, from the director who is employed because the board want a peer, to the receptionist who is employed for her shapely figure. But wherever it is possible to say that there is a job to do, it is also possible to say whether it is being done well or badly. There is an "acceptable standard" of results, the "end" to which human qualities are merely "means". It is these results which must be written into the job objectives.

The job objectives of a manager include the job objectives of all subordinates, to be achieved through them. If there is a failure, both have failed, and must discuss the reasons and overcome the failure together.

If the job objectives are all known, and precisely measured, subordinates may know how they are doing without being told. The interview in their case will summarise this knowledge, taking a bird's-eye view; discuss the reasons for any unexpected or significant results; and plan the future. But often subordinates will not know how they are doing until they are told, because some of the relevant facts or judgements are available first to their boss.

10. Preparation

The most important and difficult part of the preparation is to establish how much ground one interview can usefully cover; and, given that time and nervous energy are limited, what to include and what to leave out. Let this decision establish the "scope" of the interview.

Many authorities hold that it is unwise to discuss salary or promotion, or to set targets or objectives for the future, in the progress interview. These matters take so much time and energy that other points will be crowded out. At the same time, the subordinate will often feel that these are a natural follow-up from a discussion about progress. The boss must therefore decide in advance of the interview what to do. If they are to be excluded from this interview, when are they to be discussed? The subordinate must know at the beginning of the progress interview what matters are ruled out and why, and refer these matters to a later occasion.

The subordinate needs to prepare too and may need help in this. Many employers invite subordinates to put down in writing, perhaps on an official form, their own interests, difficulties, needs, successes, ambitions, questions, and suggestions. Further, it may be useful for boss and subordinate to give each other, a week or two before the interview, one or two items for the agenda. Both can then think about these items in advance.

11. Structure

The structure, or sequence, of the progress interview will again depend on what it is to include, and which of the aims it will serve. It is worth emphasising that there is no one universally correct type of progress interview; but whatever the type, the interviewer must define the purpose and outline the scope and limits of the interview early on.

There is, however, one problem common to most interviewers. If there are good points and bad, which should come first? The natural inclination of the interviewer is to take the good points first. They are the least "troublesome" (though they can cause trouble when the subordinate disagrees with the boss on their importance). They give the boss time to get on the subordinate's wavelength. They help to put the subordinate at ease.

Against this method there are two arguments:

1. The subordinate will be waiting mainly for anything critical. If all the good points come first, they may not be heard; the subordinate is working out what the criticisms are.

2. It is important to end on a "good note".

The best answer may well be to have a careful and, if necessary, long introduction to the interview. This should not only describe the purposes and scope, as already indicated, but give the structure of the interview, indicating that the strengths of the subordinate will be discussed after the weaknesses. Moreover, the introduction should include some reassurance that the overall assessment is satisfactory. Normally either the performance and results are, broadly, satisfactory, or they are unsatisfactory and the structure of the reprimand interview is more appropriate.

Where there is a firmly square peg in an unchangeable round hole, neither congratulation nor reprimand is in order. Something has gone wrong with the selection procedure. It will probably be important to emphasise that the mistake is not the fault of the victim, and in the interests of both parties the subordinate must find a more suitable job. Such an introduction should lead naturally on to a constructive (though not agreeable) interview.

Planning a careful structure is vital in this interview; the temptation to digress is powerful, and sometimes a digression is a valuable way of relaxing, of standing back from the interview, of renewing strength before the next problem. But the boss must know that it is a digression and be able to bring the conversation back. There is nothing like an intermediate summing up for this purpose.

12. Conclusion

The progress interview takes different forms, all of them difficult. It represents in highly concentrated form the whole art of management. If it succeeds, it is a powerful way of leading, managing and serving an individual subordinate. It has many drawbacks and pitfalls, and can easily fail.

For the interview, manager and subordinate have to leave their social relationship and concentrate on the work, and the way work brings them together and separates them. But this change of relationship, of "hats", may have to be done slowly and carefully, so that the subordinate is not given a jolt, and so that the social relationship is preserved whatever happens in the interview.

All emotion should be drained away. The "putting at ease" must include an attempt to assess how much fear and anger there may be in the mind of the subordinate. Such emotions have to be allayed or harnessed to the purposes of the interview, or they will obstruct those purposes. If they are brought into the open early on, and the subordinate is allowed to speak at length, it is more likely that the progress interview proper will go forward rationally. Where the problems are too severe, or complicated, to be merely part of the "putting at ease" process, probably the progress interview will have to be postponed and a grievance interview held instead.

Many of the problems and drawbacks can be overcome by the boss passing the initiative for the agenda to the subordinate. All of us do judge ourselves continually, though often incorrectly, so the only skill involved is in persuading the subordinate to think out loud. People will not tell the whole truth of their own assessment;

who ever tells the whole truth in the presence of their boss? And the boss should not expect it. But if the interview is successful, it should benefit the subordinate. It may as well start from the subordinate's point of view.

Progress interviews which are compulsory, by order of the employer, start at a disadvantage. "Well, Fred, you will no doubt have heard on the grapevine that we all have to discuss and appraise the progress of each subordinate at this interview." Although in the long run many organisations have derived benefit from a system introduced in this way, like any other activity that people do under pressure, it is liable to cause resentment.

It is as if people were under an obligation to smile; most of us prefer to do these things at our own pace.

The work itself should be justification for some kind of progress interview, but the kind of interview which the work requires may not accord with the employer's legislation.

Occasionally a special interview might not seem to serve any purpose, and if neither boss nor subordinate can see any point, it is better not to hold the interview, unless the employer's legislation requires it.

Nobody can do a managerial job well without conducting progress interviews, any more than without giving orders or keeping discipline. A good manager starts with some native wit in interviewing, reinforced by training and classroom practice in giving progress interviews, and before each interview prepares thoroughly.

13. Summary notes

Aims
1. To improve individual performance by recognition and guidance
2. To reconcile the individual's own ambitions with the employer's objectives

Preparation
1. Study the job objectives.
2. Analyse the achievement of each objective
3. Consider the individual's potential; whether this person is being fully "stretched"; what changes could be made so that the job

would use the person's full capacity
4. Consider the forms of recognition and reward open, apart from private congratulation at the interview:
    (a) financial
    (b) promotion
    (c) privileges
    (d) extra responsibility or assistance
    (e) training
5. Plan the progress interview in relation to the individual's long-term development, and the development of the organisation
6. Avoid holding the interview at a time of crisis
7. Give at least a week's notice of the forthcoming interview, and invite the subordinate to prepare for it.

Structure
 1. Put at ease
 2. State the nature of the interview
 3. Give an overall impression of work and progress
 4. Outline the structure of the interview
 5. Get understanding of the purpose of the interview
 6. Get agreement on the main job objectives, and the achievements of each objective
 7. Discuss where improvement is possible, and how. Training?
 8. Discuss strengths, and points for congratulation
 9. Discuss ambitions and enthusiasms
10. Any questions?
11. Sum up (in a job-centred and impersonal way)
12. Get agreement on job objectives for the next six to twelve months
13. Arrange the date of the next progress interview
14. End on a note of confidence, trust and satisfaction.

Check results
 1. Watch the points raised for improvement, and congratulate if appropriate
 2. Check performance in the job generally
 3. Check relations and attitude
 4. Prepare for the next progress interview.

Chapter 5
Role-Plays

1. How to role-play

1. The roles marked "a" are for the boss, who should control the progress of the interview. The interview is held at the request of a, except grievance interviews, which are at b's request.

2. The tutor gives a role to each player. Players do not know what is in their opposite number's role. Sometimes it is helpful to give both the players the same information, or to allow them to exchange information before the role-play begins. But separate roles are usually better, as the interviewer is forced to probe for information and deal with unexpected twists in the dialogue.

3. Players are free to invent what facts they like, compatible with their own role. In theory their inventions might be incompatible with one another, leading to a stalemate, but this seldom happens.

4. Remember the purpose of these role-plays is to practise the principles described, not to show off. Players and observers usually learn more from an interview that fails than from one that succeeds.

5. Players always want more information than they receive. The more information, the more life-like the role seems. But several pages take a long time to read and are difficult to remember, and the realism is even then an illusion. Tutors should settle for the briefest role that will allow the player to apply what has been learnt.

6. If the tutor can rewrite these skeleton roles using terms and difficulties familiar to the players, they will be more successful. All roles can be played by a man or a woman.

7. Tape-recorders and closed circuit television are useful aids. They enable the tutor to replay and analyse the interview in detail, and the participants to see the "meaning" of pause, speed, tone, volume, position, gesture, etc. After the players have got over the first shock of hearing and seeing themselves as others do, the replay will improve their performance and confidence.

8. Roles in selection and progress (appraisal) interviews may be played more thoroughly if time allows, using such records as application forms or assessment forms which the real interview requires.

9. It is good fun writing your own role-plays, but if the game is to be educational make sure the roles illustrate at least one specific difficulty. On the other hand, avoid putting in too many teaching points, or none of them will emerge clearly. In my experience, the simplest role-play often yields the richest harvest of points for discussion.

2. Sample role-plays

Role-play 1

(a) You have a personal assistant due to be transferred to Head Office in 12 months or so. You have a vacancy for a clerk at the moment. The successful clerk will be responsible to the personal assistant, but will have to work independently when you and the personal assistant are at conferences, and at holiday times, and when there is sickness. Possibly a good applicant could succeed the personal assistant in due course. Interview an applicant.

(b) You are a candidate for a clerical vacancy. For the last two years you have had a boring routine job in the Invoicing Department as a junior clerk. You want a job with more initiative. You are 22 years old, with five O levels and one A level (geography). At school you organised the School Fair (a fund-raising day) and edited the school magazine. You are the eldest of four children. Do not volunteer any information.

Role-play 2

(a) Play the role of your present job. You have to welcome to your team a new employee, aged 18. She is said to be a recruit of promise, who deserves training and development. It is her first working day with your organisation, and you have to tell her whatever she ought to know, or wants to know, on that day. She will report directly to you.

(b) You are aged 18. You have joined this organisation as a poor second best to going to university (where you could not secure a place). You want to continue your education if possible in the new job, about which you know little in detail. You are shy and reluctant to talk in strange surroundings.

Role-play 3

(a) You are a manager in charge of several offices. In one the senior clerk, Wiggins, had a breakdown two months ago and went to hospital. It was uncertain if he would return. You were lucky to get the services of an efficient replacement, who runs his office superbly. Your own boss now tells you that Wiggins has recovered and will be back in a fortnight, and that the replacement will also be remaining with you. You decide to tell the replacement that Wiggins is returning.

(b) You were brought in as an office supervisor two months ago when your predecessor, Mr. Wiggins, had a breakdown and went to hospital. The office works well and you enjoy it. No one has told you whether Wiggins is to return, or what happens to you if he does. The boss sends for you.

Role-play 4

(a) You are the supervisor of a word processor installation. You have put a new operator, who started with you yesterday with experience of a similar system, on to prepare some invoices. You have been keeping an eye on the work, and have just found that two piles of invoices have been printed with the customer code missing. Speak about it.

(b) You started work yesterday in a word processor installation responsible for processing invoices. After experience on a more old-fashioned system, you have just been put on to automatic invoicing. It looked simple enough, but your supervisor has just come up to you and found that there's something missing on your invoices. Play the role as though you were flustered, annoyed with yourself, and will be angry if your supervisor should make any unjustified criticism.

Role-play 5

(a) You have been made head of a small section that keeps statistical records. The section is efficient and morale is high but timekeeping is poor. The hours are nine to five; no flexitime. Last week a senior manager advised you not to let timekeeping get slack; it "let the side down, and made it difficult for other managers to keep their staff up to the mark". You decide to speak to a junior member of staff who is practically never on time and who was 20 minutes late this morning.

(b) You are a junior of a small and happy section that keeps statistical records. You have just passed your driving test and have bought a car. You have joined a group of drivers who live near you and work at the same establishment, and take turns to drive each other in. One of the group is a senior scientist who is not much concerned with punctuality; this morning, for instance, he drove you in and you were 15 minutes late. The hours are nine to five; no flexitime. The section has recently got a new boss who you are afraid may demand punctuality. The boss has sent for you.

Role-play 6

(a) You are the safety officer. You have gone into a workshop and found someone working the guillotine without putting the guard in position. You caught the same person doing this last week and gave a verbal warning. The excuse was that the guard held up the work, but you pointed out that it was a safety regulation. You feel the time has come for a reprimand.

(b) The safety officer found you in your workshop using the guillotine without the safety guard last week, and warned you that this was against the regulations. But you resent the guard, which slows down the work and reduces your bonus. As the safety officer is not your boss, you need not take much notice; you can't work for two bosses, and your own supervisor turns a blind eye. Now the safety officer has caught you a second time.

Role-play 7

(a) You are a personnel manager. You have to conduct a progress interview with an assistant personnel officer Jo, whose work has been reliable but unimaginative. Jo gets on well with the other members of the department, and is a balanced individual. You might be able to think about promotion next year, if Jo showed more enthusiasm for modern ideas in personnel management. Jo would also be well advised to know the staff better, and their problems.

(b) You are an assistant personnel officer, due to have your progress interview. Your spouse has been ill lately, and the worry of that and looking after your three children as well as the job has been difficult. You have not talked about it much because you do not think it is your employer's business. You know you have not put much effort into your work, partly for fear of being given a lot of the extra documentation the organisation now requires, but you want to give a good impression at the interview.

Role-play 8
(a) You are a plant manager, about to give one of your supervisors a progress interview. Since she joined your organisation her record has been good, until lately. She has been unwilling to cooperate with the work study team going round the plant, and the team has hardly been able to obtain any accurate measurements of the work of her section. Other supervisors are not so unreasonable, and you want to change her attitude to be more like theirs. Work study is an important part of the management's plan to contain costs and keep competitive; they have given assurances that no one will lose their jobs as a result of work study.

(b) You are a supervisor going for a progress interview with your plant manager. You have been worried by the work study team which has lately been trying to measure the work of your section. You were declared redundant from your last job five years ago after a similar work study campaign, and (despite management promises that no one will lose their job) you think the campaign is intended to make the staff work harder for less pay, and eventually reduce the number on the payroll. You have therefore advised your subordinates to go slow when their work is being measured.

Role-play 9
(a) You are manager of an assembly plant for motor accessories. Yesterday you spent some time meeting shop stewards, discussing a possible new bonus incentive scheme. It has always been your policy to take the shop stewards into your confidence early on, and get them to put proposals to the shop floor; you think this saves time in the long run. But it has put you behind with your normal work. Your oldest supervisor has asked to see you, and although you have a lot to do, you agree.

b) You are a supervisor in an assembly plant. You have been angry for some time with your plant manager, who seems to tell everything to the shop stewards before telling you. Today your steward is full of a new bonus incentive scheme that the manager discussed yesterday. To preserve your own authority you pretended to know something about it, and you ask to see the boss, to find out about the scheme, and to have a real row about the way you are kept in the dark.

Role-play 10
(a) You are the works manager. In the recent batch of promotions to foreman, one of your older workers has been passed by. This is the result of a new policy which replaces promotion according to seniority by promotion of those of more recent technical education, and requires the promotion of younger men so that the organisation can get longer service from them, and perhaps promote them higher. Your "senior citizen" has asked to see you.

(b) You are in your late forties and were expected to be promoted foreman on seniority. You have heard rumours of a new policy, but didn't realise what it meant until you were passed over in the latest batch of promotions. You are very angry about this, since you can do any job in the shop better than any of the younger operators. You have asked to see your works manager to see what is going on.

Role-play 11
(a) You are a storekeeper with two clerks working for you. One of them is on leave. The other takes lunch late, with your permission, and usually has sandwiches in the office. An engineer has come to see you with a complaint. Your staff tell you that this engineer asks for items of equipment which are not usually kept in stock, and when they are available, no longer wants them.

(b) You are an engineer and have gone to the storekeeper to complain about the attitude of the staff in the store. They are ignorant and unhelpful. Shortly after lunch you went to get some valves, and the person in the office, reading a paper, said "Help yourself" without looking up. You couldn't find what you wanted, and the only comment you got was "Perhaps we're out of stock."

Role-play 12

(a) You are head of a small information department. One of your best workers, a graduate aged 24 who is good at abstracting, has suddenly given notice and is due to leave next week. You cannot discover why. You were away when the bombshell dropped, but you are back in the department now. You feel there is something wrong and ask for a final chat.

(b) You are a graduate aged 24. You joined the organisation six months ago, hoping for a progressive job. You are in a small information department, doing boring and routine work with no prospects. You have given notice and are leaving next week. Your boss, who was away when you gave notice, always tries to jolly you along instead of listening to your complaints. If you receive a sympathetic hearing, you could suggest that in future they treat graduates with respect, give them more responsibility (allow them to deal with outsiders without supervision, for example), talk to them about their progress and prospects, and welcome their suggestions. Don't bother saying all this unless you are properly asked.

Role-play 13

(a) You are a manager responsible for the work of a commercial records section whose supervisor is leaving in a month's time. This supervisor has asked to see you. Part of the problem is no doubt tying up the job before the supervisor goes. Another problem might be Mr Smith, who shares the office and telephone. Mr Smith's job is to chase up supplies, so he spends a lot of time on the telephone. When he was transferred to you last month there was no proper office for him to go to, so you had to put him with the commercial records people.

(b) You are the supervisor of a commercial records section, but leaving in a month's time. Most of the job you hand over to your successor will be straightforward, but a new man, Mr Smith, is a bit of a headache. He shares your room and telephone although he is not in your section. He spends most of the day on the telephone talking to suppliers, and affecting the concentration and morale of your section. You ask to see the manager to press him to find Mr. Smith another place.

Role-play 14

(a) You are in charge of a research laboratory. You have had an assistant, Jo, aged 20, working for you for about six months. Jo does not seem stupid, but has to be told what to do all the time. You have ticked Jo off twice for starting a process without completing the safety procedures, and twice for not getting on with the job. Give Jo a progress interview.

(b) You are a laboratory assistant aged 20. You have been working for your present boss for about six months. The section does not seem to be very busy and frequently you do not have enough to do. Your boss has twice spotted that you started a process before the safety procedures were complete, and has nagged you a couple of times for not working fast enough. You are worried about your gambling debts: you now owe about six months' salary to various friends, but your boss does not (you hope) know about this yet.

3. Comments on each role-play

1. The boss should not say anything which could be construed as promise of promotion. The applicant may not be suitable; the personal assistant's transfer may not come through. If a promise made at a selection interview is broken, you have an embittered employee on your hands.

2. At this interview bosses tend to talk too much and listen too little. New recruits take in little on their first day.

3. Before the interview the boss must take a firm decision, probably that Wiggins will be in charge on returning, and communicate this unpleasant fact clearly in the interview.

4. As the operator is new, explanation and encouragement are needed, not anger, however annoying the mistake is.

5. The latecomer must agree with the boss on the facts of the lateness and the conditions of employment, and accept a duty to reconcile the two. If the boss can give help or advice, so much the better. But the car, other late employees, the senior scientist and the actual number of minutes late, are all "red herrings".

6. Only a person's superior can effectively give a reprimand. The safety officer should have some sanctions (reporting, etc) and know what they are.

7. The personnel manager should be able to uncover the home background, and may go on to inspire the assistant to develop an interest in the work; but if the home problems have spoiled the atmosphere for discussing work, that discussion should be postponed to a later interview.

8. The plant manager should question the supervisor to elicit the strength of feeling. It may be worth admitting that the work study campaign has not been properly explained. The boss could suggest a meeting between the work study staff and all the supervisors, to discuss how all can benefit from the campaign.

9. The manager should welcome this complaint as a chance to correct an important and common failing: by-passing the supervisor. The interview should discuss how to prevent it happening again, but this must be managerial policy, not an abdication of power.

10. Management have not communicated a change in promotion policy, and the works manager is taking the consequences. Logically, the new policy should help the organisation directly, and indirectly the present victim. But logic will not heal wounded pride; the interview is easier to conduct if the victim can be found a new job, well away from those who know about the missed promotion. If the new job has an impressive title, so much the better.

11. Bosses should not admit their staff have behaved badly before hearing their side of the story.

12. This interview should give constructive feedback affecting selection policy (not recruiting people too well qualified for the job), the selection interview (warning recruits about a job's snags), and human relations after recruitment.

13. The boss should collect and record the facts; judge them; decide whether to confirm them (perhaps by staying for a time in the office); and if the problem is correctly stated, pass it to someone who can solve it.

14. If the gambling problem is not to interfere with the person's work, the boss must uncover it, question and listen with sympathy, and either work out a solution jointly with the gambler, or pass it to a personnel or welfare officer to deal with. Objectively the

problem is easy to cope with, once the frightened victim is not trying to solve it alone.

4. Role-play check list

The purpose of listening carefully to an interview and assessing its progress is to help the interviewer to recognise how it looks to an outsider, and so master the principles and techniques, and to provide the basis for discussing, analysing and learning from the interview after it is over.

Discussion is much more fruitful if you attach your comments to specific words or phrases. Do not try to cover every point below; it is better to make a detailed observation on one or two.

1. Opening
Was the atmosphere created at the beginning helpful?
Was the transition from greeting to business a smooth one?
Did the interviewee understand the kind of interview it was, and its purpose?

2. Structure
Was the structure suitable for this interview?
Was the interview long enough?
Did the interviewer put the case clearly? Keep control of the interview?
Ask for questions?
Listen enough?
Sum up after each main point, and at the end?

3. Style
Were the words well chosen for this particular interviewee?
Was the interviewer sincere? Friendly and polite?
Did the interviewer show self-control?
Was the degree of participation satisfactory?
Were relationships good for the purpose of the interview?

4. Ending
Was the interview well summarised?
Were differences of opinion fairly treated?

Did the parties agree on a conclusion?
Was it clear what was to happen next?
Were the agreed conclusion and action tied in to the purpose of
the interview, as stated at the opening?
Was the interview good "public relations" for management?
What, of permanent value, did the interview achieve?

Appendices

Appendix A
Equal Opportunities Commission: Code of Practice

Extracts relating to recruitment and discipline

Introduction

1. The Equal Opportunities Commission (EOC) issues this Code of Practice for the following reasons:

(a) for the elimination of discrimination in employment;
(b) to give guidance as to what steps it is reasonably practicable for employers to take to ensure that their employees do not in the course of their employment act unlawfully contrary to the Sex Discrimination Act (SDA);
(c) for the promotion of equality of opportunity between men and women in employment.

The SDA prohibits discrimination against men, as well as against women. It also requires that married people should not be treated less favourably than single people of the same sex.

Recruitment

12. It is unlawful, unless the job is covered by an exception, to discriminate directly or indirectly on the grounds of sex or marriage

- in the arrangements for deciding who should be offered a job;
- in any terms of employment;
- by refusing or omitting to offer a person employment.

13. It is therefore recommended that:

(a) each individual should be assessed according to his or her personal capability to carry out a given job. It should not be assumed that men only or women only will be able to perform certain kinds of work;

(b) any qualifications or requirements applied to a job which effectively inhibit applications from one sex or from married people should be retained only if they are justifiable in terms of the job to be done;

(c) any age limits should be retained only if they are necessary for the job. An unjustifiable age limit could constitute unlawful indirect discrimination, for example, against women who have taken time out of employment for child-rearing; ...

Selection methods

22. It is unlawful: unless the job is covered by an exception, to discriminate on grounds of sex or marriage by refusing or deliberately omitting to offer employment.

23. It is therefore recommended that:

(a) employers should ensure that personnel staff, line managers and all other employees, who may come into contact with job applicants, should be trained in the provisions of the SDA, including the fact that it is unlawful to instruct or put pressure on others to discriminate;

(b) applications from men and women should be processed in exactly the same way. For example, there should not be separate lists of male and female or married and single applicants. All those handling applications and conducting interviews should be trained in the avoidance of unlawful discrimination and records of interviews kept, where practicable, showing why applicants were or were not appointed;

(c) questions should relate to the requirements of the job. Where it is necessary to assess whether personal circumstances will affect performance of the job (for example, where it involves unsocial hours or extensive travel) this should be discussed objectively without detailed questions based on assumptions about marital status, children and domestic obligations. Questions about marriage plans or family intentions should not be asked, as they could be construed as showing bias against women. Information necessary for personal records can be collected after a job offer has been made.

Grievances, disciplinary procedures and victimisation
30. It is unlawful: to victimise an individual for a complaint made in good faith about sex or marriage discrimination or for giving evidence about such a complaint.

Dismissals, redundancies and other unfavourable treatment of employees
32. It is unlawful: to discriminate directly or indirectly on grounds of sex or marriage in dismissals or by treating an employee unfavourably in any other way.

It is therefore recommended that:

(a) care is taken that members of one sex are not disciplined or dismissed for performance which would be overlooked or condoned in the other sex;
(b) redundancy procedures affecting a group of employees predominantly of one sex should be reviewed, so as to remove any effects which would be disproportionate and unjustifiable; ...
(c) all reasonably practical steps should be taken to ensure that a standard of conduct or behaviour is observed which prevents members of either sex from being intimidated, harassed or otherwise subjected to unfavourable treatment on the ground of their sex.

Formulating an equal opportunities policy
34. An equal opportunities policy will ensure the effective use of human resources in the best interests of both the organisation and its employees. It is a commitment by an employer to the development and use of employment procedures and practices which do not discriminate on grounds of sex or marriage and which provide genuine equality of opportunity for all employees.

Monitoring
39. In a large and complex organisation a more formal analysis [than in a small one] will be necessary, for example, by sex, grade, and payment of each unit. This may need to be introduced by stages as resources permit. Any formal analysis should be regularly updated and available to management and trade unions

to enable any necessary action to be taken.

40. Sensible monitoring will show, for example, whether members of one sex:

(a) do not apply for employment or promotion, or that fewer apply than might be expected;
(b) are not recruited, promoted or selected for training and development or are appointed/selected in a significantly lower proportion than their rate of application;
(c) are concentrated in certain jobs, sections or departments.

Positive action
41. Selection for recruitment or promotion must be on merit, irrespective of sex. However, the Sex Discrimination Act does allow certain steps to redress the effects of previous unequal opportunities. Where there have been few or no members of one sex in particular work in their employment for the previous 12 months, the Act allows employers to give special encouragement to, and provide specific training for, the minority sex. Such measures are usually described as positive discrimination.

Appendix B
Commission for Racial Equality: Code of Practice

Extracts relating to recruitment

1.14 In order to avoid direct or indirect discrimination it is recommended that:
(a) gate, reception and personnel staff should be instructed not to treat casual or formal applicants from particular racial groups less favourably than others. These instructions should be confirmed in writing:
(b) in addition, staff responsible for shortlisting, interviewing and selecting candidates should be:

- clearly informed of selection criteria and of the need for consistent application;
- given guidance or training on the effects which generalised assumptions and prejudices about race can have on selection decisions;
- made aware of the possible misunderstandings that occur in interviews between persons of different cultural backgrounds;

(c) wherever possible, shortlisting and interviewing should not be done by one person alone but should at least be checked at a more senior level.

1.38 Except in cases where there are large numbers of applicants and the burden on resources would be excessive, reasons for selection and rejection should be recorded at each stage of the selection process, eg initial shortlisting and final decisions. Simple categories of reasons for rejection should be adequate for the early sifting stage.

1.41 Is there evidence that individuals from any particular racial group:

(a) do not apply for employment or promotion, or that fewer apply than might be expected?

(b) are not recruited or promoted at all, or are appointed in a significantly lower proportion than their rate of application?

(c) are under-represented in training or in jobs carrying higher pay, status or authority?

(d) are concentrated in certain shifts, sections or departments?

Further Reading from Kogan Page

The Business Fact Finder, ed. Hano Johannsen
Don't Do. Delegate! The Secret Power of Successful Managers,
    James M Jenks and John M Kelly
Effective Performance Appraisals, Robert B Maddux
Essential Management Checklists, Jeffrey P Davidson
A Handbook of Management Techniques, Michael Armstrong
How To Be an Even Better Manager, Michael Armstrong
How To Make Meetings Work, Malcolm Peel
Winning Strategies for Managing People: A Task Directed Guide,
    Robert Irwin and Rita Wolenik

Index